SUCCESSFUL MATHEMATICS LEADERSHIP IN PRIMARY SCHOOLS

Successful Mathematics Leadership in Primary Schools: the role of the mathematics co-ordinator

Gina Donaldson

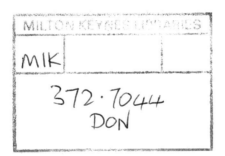

Learning Matters

First published in 2002 by Learning Matters Ltd.

British Library Cataloguing in Publication Data
A CIP record for this book is available from the British Library.

ISBN 1 903300 46 0

Cover design by Topics – The Creative Partnership
Project management by Deer Park Productions
Typeset by PDQ Typesetting
Printed and bound by Bell & Bain Ltd., Glasgow

Learning Matters Ltd
58 Wonford Road
Exeter EX2 4LQ
Tel: 01392 215560
info@learningmatters.co.uk
www.learningmatters.co.uk

CONTENTS

'Subject leaders provide professional leadership and management for a subject to secure high quality teaching, effective use of resources and improved standards of learning and achievement for all pupils'

(DfES, 2001)

Schools are constantly asked to review their practices and raise standards. Subject leaders play a key role in this process of developing effective teaching and learning. Although professional leadership from the head and deputy teacher is essential, there is a wealth of expertise to be developed through other members of staff, who might be thought of as teachers who lead from the middle. From this position, subject leaders are actively involved with the everyday life of the school and can lead the implementation of changes from their own classrooms.

Subject leaders are generally class teachers who may have been teaching for several years, who are reflective classroom practitioners and who are beginning to gain an insight into whole school issues. This follows the significant shift of thinking from the newly qualified teacher's focus on the classroom to an awareness of wider issues. As subject leaders, these members of staff represent a potentially powerful force. 'Subject leader' and 'co-ordinator' are used synonymously in this book, but I have chosen to use the term 'subject leader' as it matches the Department for Education and Skills (DfES) description of the role in *The Teachers' Standards Framework* (DfES, 2001).

This book is written to help teachers become effective subject leaders of mathematics. You may already be appointed in this position, or be aiming to apply for such a post in the near future. Alternatively, you may be new to the teaching profession and want to gain a better understanding of the career and professional development opportunities available to you.

The role of the subject leader is many faceted. The subject leader of mathematics played an important role in the introduction of the National Numeracy Strategy (NNS) and there is still a continuing expectation that subject leaders will use professional development materials to raise standards. Furthermore, the NNS recommends that the subject leader undertakes audits of mathematics, completes self-evaluations and produces planning for professional development. This book aims to support you in this.

You are also responsible for your own professional development. This book defines the role of subject leader and supports you in the setting and meeting of realistic targets which will not only aid your continuing development but also raise standards in your school. The *Teachers' Standards Framework* offers a structure for professional development by charting pathways of progression from newly qualified teacher through to head teacher, with the role of subject leader as a possible stepping stone. Subject leaders can therefore be seen as emergent leaders.

The following ten chapters in this book aim to reflect key skills and issues, and, for ease of use, each is structured in a similar way beginning with the specific National Standards for Subject Leaders (as set out in the *Teachers' Standards Framework*) that will be addressed. Questions are included throughout to help you to reflect on your current situation and future professional development, and references to literature and research are included when these will help you develop in your role. The first two chapters suggest how you may begin to establish yourself as subject leader and to develop the effective teaching and learning of mathematics across the school. It would be useful to begin with these chapters, and to refer to later chapters which cover more specific issues as your role develops.

➔ The National Standards for Subject Leadership state that subject leaders should:

- have knowledge and understanding of the characteristics of high quality teaching and the main strategies for improving and sustaining high standards of teaching, learning and achievement for all pupils;
- evaluate the teaching of the subject in the school, use this analysis to identify effective practice and areas for improvement and take action to improve further the quality of teaching;
- monitor the progress made in achieving subject plans and targets, evaluate the effects on teaching and learning, and use this analysis to guide further improvement;
- establish staff and resource needs and advise the head teacher and senior managers of likely priorities for expenditure, and allocate available resources with maximum efficiency to meet the objectives of the school and subject plans and achieve value for money;
- create a climate which enables other staff to develop and maintain positive attitudes towards the subject and confidence in teaching it;
- take responsibility for their own professional development;
- prioritise and manage own time effectively, particularly in relation to balancing the demands made by teaching, subject management and involvement in school development;
- achieve challenging professional goals.

Reflection

What do you as a class teacher expect in terms of leadership and support from other curriculum subject leaders?

What would you like to achieve as subject leader of mathematics?

The position of mathematics subject leader is often advertised as a specific role in the school, and is sometimes accompanied by a financial reward, which suggests it is a significant position within the structure of the staff. When considering developing a career in this direction, it is useful to reflect on the role, in order to prepare yourself fully for interviews and first appointments, to identify training needs, and to set targets for professional development. So it is important for you to be able to define the role of subject leader.

The subject leader for mathematics:

- is an effective teacher of mathematics;
- is aware of current issues and developments in mathematics education;
- manages the mathematics budget and organises resources;
- demonstrates secure subject knowledge;
- monitors teaching and learning;
- sets and monitors whole school targets;
- provides written policies and guidelines;
- manages the transition between Key Stages;
- leads staff development in mathematics;
- co-ordinates inclusive practices and ensures that the needs of all children are met;
- advises on assessment issues in mathematics;
- involves parents in their children's learning.

Some of these aspects will be discussed here; others will be covered in later chapters.

An effective teacher of mathematics

It is not necessary to hold particular mathematical qualifications such as an A level or a degree to be a subject leader, although secure subject knowledge is essential. It is more important to gain respect as an effective teacher of mathematics.

Reflection

It is worth considering how teachers gain respect from each other. Reflect on one teacher you have worked alongside, and whom you would consider as an effective teacher. How do you know what sort of teacher they are? Is this information gathered through comments made in the staff room, opinions of children and parents, observation of teachers with their classes moving around the school, assemblies, displays...? Sometimes observation of a teacher interacting with children whilst on playground duty gives an insight into their relationship with individuals.

It is important for you to be able to describe the characteristics of an effective teacher of mathematics. This will help you to provide a vision of how you would like the teaching and learning of mathematics to be developed throughout the school. It will act as a benchmark as you audit, monitor and develop the current provision for mathematics.

What are the characteristics of an effective teacher of mathematics? These may include securing high standards in National Tests and formal summative tests, although most teachers would feel this is a limited measurement of teaching and learning. An effective teacher would have an ability to raise standards for all the individuals in the class. They would be creative and inspiring in their teaching, perhaps stemming from their own fascination with mathematics itself. They would offer secure foundations for a lifetime of learning of mathematics, providing meaningful mathematical experiences for children. Their teaching of mathematics would include opportunities for spiritual, cultural, social and moral development. Lessons would be exciting, motivating and intriguing.

Research projects such as Askew (1997) have tried to identify the characteristics of good mathematics teachers. This project worked with a selection of teachers, monitoring their performance by testing their classes before and after a period of teaching. They found that mathematical qualifications, specific teaching styles and the use of published resources were not necessarily significant characteristics of effective teachers. The characteristics shared by the most effective teachers were their commitment to INSET (in-service training) and the set of beliefs which underpinned their teaching of numeracy. These beliefs relate to the way in which teachers understand what it is to be numerate, and therefore determine the way in which they present mathematics to children and guide their learning. The project identified three sets of beliefs, although teachers often display characteristics of more than one set. The most effective teachers shared the view that the teaching of mathematics is not about transmitting subject knowledge or providing opportunities for children to discover mathematics: rather it is a matter of exploring the connections within mathematics with children. These teachers were themselves aware of the connections between areas of mathematics in the primary curriculum. They felt that all children are able to learn mathematics through activities which challenge them to develop and explore a network of connections. Effective teaching therefore makes connections between:

- what children know already and new concepts and skills;
- children's informal intuitive knowledge and formal mathematics;
- representations of mathematics: concrete activities, language, and symbols;
- areas of mathematics such as addition and subtraction; or fractions, decimals and percentages.

The research called this a connectionist orientation. Further information on this research can be found in Askew (1997) and Thompson (1999).

The mathematics subject leader should be able to justify their own vision of an effective teacher of mathematics, in order to lead discussions, implement changes and establish high expectations. They should also be prepared to increase the profile of mathematics, through displays, whole school mathematical events and assemblies etc. This enables the subject leader to monitor teaching and learning as well as increasing motivation and enthusiasm.

Keeping up to date with current issues and developments in mathematics education

The mathematics subject leader has a duty to be aware of current research findings, changes in thinking and new developments. These should be evaluated critically and shared with the staff, when they are relevant. The mathematics subject leader needs to read journals, government reports and educational literature. It may be possible to use the mathematics budget to buy subscriptions for the two main professional associations: The Mathematical Association www.m-a.org.uk and The Association of Teachers of Mathematics www.atm.org.uk. The website www.standards.dfes.gov.uk/numeracy is an excellent source of information and resources.

Managing the mathematics budget and organising resources

The size of the mathematics budget allocation can vary according to the number of areas of the curriculum undergoing development at any one time. Sponsorship, and events run by the children or Parents Association, can supplement budgets when a specific purchase is needed. Subject leaders are accountable to their colleagues, the head teacher, parents, governors and the Office for Standards in Education (OFSTED) when making decisions on the spending of budgets. Therefore decisions should be made after collecting and considering relevant information. This will be discussed at a later stage.

The subject leader is responsible for ensuring appropriate use of resources, and for organising those resources, which may be centrally or in classrooms. Storage of resources centrally is more economical for small schools, but generally requires the subject leader to keep the area tidied. In some cases the subject leader may find that resources stored centrally are not often used. Storage in classrooms requires more resources to be purchased, but enables teachers and children to access them more independently. Often schools keep some of the more specialised and large equipment centrally whilst the rest is kept within classrooms.

How will subject leaders become aware of the way in which resources are used in classrooms other than their own? For example, a subject leader would want to ensure that capacity containers were used appropriately, not for storing paint brushes! Central storage of resources enables subject leaders to monitor their use more closely. Scrutiny of class teachers' weekly planning can also provide monitoring information. The subject leader will need to establish opportunities to discuss the use of resources, perhaps informally or during staff meetings and INSET sessions.

Demonstrating secure subject knowledge

The subject leader acts as a source of knowledge for the staff, providing support in answering subject related questions, planning lessons that address rather than contribute to misconceptions, ensuring the correct use of mathematical vocabulary and provision for able children. The subject leader may not necessarily commit this information to memory, but needs to have easy access to this sort of information through a good bank of materials.

Monitoring teaching and learning

This is a difficult role, and requires non-contact time if it is to be done effectively. Many schools have a policy of releasing subject leaders to observe and work with colleagues in their classrooms. Classroom observation and any written notes made during or after the observation need to be handled sensitively. Issues relating to classroom observation will be covered in a later chapter. To a certain extent, monitoring teaching can take place through a scrutiny of medium-term and weekly planning, classroom displays, assessment records, samples of children's work or through informal talk in the staff room. This can give a subject leader an insight into the content and organisation of lessons, use of resources etc, and provide valuable information when planning development of teaching and learning.

Reflection

You might find it useful to discuss aspects of this role with a practising mathematics subject leader. The following questions might be used to structure the discussion:

- *How does the subject leader monitor teaching and learning across the school?*
- *Does the school have a subject development plan for mathematics?*
- *How are staff development needs identified and catered for?*
- *How are budgets allocated?*
- *How are resources managed?*
- *How does the subject leader become aware of up to date issues?*
- *Does the subject leader have a role in monitoring the provision for children with additional learning needs?*
- *How does the subject leader ensure secure subject knowledge amongst the staff?*
- *Does the subject leader have a role in assessment?*
- *How are whole school standards monitored, and does the subject leader have a role in whole school target setting?*
- *Is test data used to monitor standards and to set whole school targets?*
- *How are policies and guidelines formulated?*
- *How is the transition between Key Stages managed?*

Beginning the role of the subject leader: the subject audit

On appointment as a subject leader, you may feel that you are expected to make some changes immediately. You yourself may feel the need to make your mark.

However, many aspects of the role rely on your knowledge of the teaching and learning of mathematics already taking place across the school, just as assessment informs planning in the classroom. I would therefore strongly recommend conducting an audit in order to gather information that will empower you to make effective changes when these are necessary. The National Numeracy Strategy also recommends that you conduct such an audit, followed by a professional action plan, and details of their advice on the audit are given on www.standards.dfes.gov.uk/numeracy.

The sorts of information you might find useful could include:

- the current mathematics policy and any other related documentation such as the marking policy, inclusion policy, and assessment policy;
- previous OFSTED inspection reports;
- National Tests data, the Qualifications and Curriculum Authority (QCA) optional test scores, and teacher assessments;
- data from your school's Performance and Assessment (Panda) Report;
- staff attitudes to the teaching of mathematics;
- staff expectations of their classes;
- head teacher's expectations and views;
- views of the governor with responsibility for mathematics;
- staff confidence in and levels of subject knowledge;
- scrutiny of long-term, medium-term and weekly planning;
- lesson observations;
- scrutiny of assessment records;
- audit of resources and books;
- views of the staff on the use of published schemes;
- use of information and communications technology (ICT) in mathematics;
- samples of children's work;
- views of LSAs (learning support assistants, teaching assistants or classroom assistants);
- views of children;
- views of parents;
- OFSTED's evaluations of the national implementation of the NNS available on www.ofsted.gov.uk.

An audit of this sort of information can be repeated regularly, in order to monitor teaching and learning. However, information should be collected in such a way as to begin a professional dialogue with colleagues which will allow you to act as a leader. This professional dialogue will be a vital tool for your role in monitoring the current provision and raising standards. It will allow you to work with staff to share your ideas and beliefs. An open relationship with colleagues allows less confident teachers to approach you for advice, and for you to deal openly with conflict should this arise.

When changes need to be implemented, these can be negotiated rather than imposed, and you will be in a position to support teachers whilst sustaining developments, rather than implementing skin-deep improvements. A newly appointed subject leader can in some cases be seen as a threat. For example, you may not feel you are in a position to ask teachers to record on paper areas of concern in their own subject knowledge. This requires a certain amount of trust. However, some information can be gathered through informal talk in the staff room, if you are able to initiate professional dialogue in an appropriate way. You will want to establish a relationship with staff where informal talk is seen not as a way of identifying weaknesses which will then be reported to the senior management team, but as an opportunity to be open about classroom practice. Similarly classroom observations can be seen as threatening. The school may have a policy for observations and these may be an accepted part of staff development, with an agreed expectation for written records of the observation. If not, it is unwise to insist on observations before a secure working relationship is established between the subject leader and the staff. Working with a teacher in their classroom, perhaps supporting individual children, or trying out new resources or teaching styles together, can be negotiated. Alternatively staff can be invited to observe the subject leader's lessons, which can lead into discussion. The subject leader should not be portrayed as the infallible expert, rather as a good practitioner with a special interest in mathematics. It is worth being open with your colleagues about your own weaknesses and failures, whilst showing yourself to be a reflective practitioner, prepared to evaluate current practice and new ideas. Establishing this position is essential to enable further development.

Development planning

Information gathered through an audit can be used to celebrate achievement and prioritise areas for development in order to draw up an action or development plan. This should be shared with the senior management of the school, as it should be incorporated in the School Development or Improvement Plan. The NNS suggests a format for development planning in their course for mathematics co-ordinators and the audit described on the Standards website. The school may also have requirements for a format of a subject development plan, but the sample plan on page 10 is one possible structure.

The subject development plan acts as a basis for allocating budgets and organising staff development. Targets should be SMART (specific, measurable, achievable, realistic and timed) and the plan should be flexible. For example, during your audit of the current provision for mathematics, you might notice that the resources for teaching capacity are rather old and dated. The teacher assessments recorded for last year might show a dip in shape, space and measures. Informal staff room talk might have also identified this as an area that some teachers do not enjoy teaching. This evidence may lead you to include the teaching of capacity as an area to address on your subject development plan. You may be able to use some of the money available for mathematics to purchase new resources and spend some time during a staff meeting discussing how these resources could be used, sharing ideas for activities, strategies for assessment and classroom organisation. You might then evaluate the success of

Target	Action	Who is responsible?	Training and staff development	Cost	Evaluation	Date to be completed

Sample subject development plan

your input by monitoring teachers' weekly plans, and by asking them to evaluate their success in using the resources at a later date. Continued support can be given to members of staff through training courses, purchasing of teachers' books or collaborative work in the classroom. However, it is important that the staff themselves are committed to making changes. This relies heavily on your ability to project your ideas of the characteristics of effective teaching of mathematics.

A target for the development plan does not necessarily have to stem from a perceived problem. You may during your gathering of information find that one member of staff is particularly effective in their use of assessment and record keeping in mathematics. You might persuade that colleague to provide feedback to the rest of the staff as part of the development of the subject. Training does not have to be delivered by you, and in fact training by other members of the staff can be particularly effective in establishing a mathematical professional dialogue. The next chapter will consider how staff development can be used to raise standards in the teaching and learning of mathematics.

Summary

Subject leaders are expected to raise standards. A full audit of current practices in your school can allow you to analyse and develop teaching and learning. Monitoring mathematics purely through National Tests results can give a limited picture, and certainly does not provide you with the knowledge and understanding of current practices throughout your school that you will need if you are going to raise standards. If your school's percentage of children reaching level 4 at the end of Key Stage 2 is low, you must certainly ensure this is addressed. But you must also ask, why are the children not reaching level 4? A full audit, which looks further than data collected from National Tests, enables you to provide full professional action planning which will direct your development of the teaching and learning of mathematics.

2 LEADING STAFF DEVELOPMENT

The National Standards for Subject Leadership state that subject leaders should:

- lead professional development through example and support, and co-ordinate the provision of high quality professional development by methods such as coaching, drawing on other sources of expertise as necessary, for example, higher education, LEAs and subject associations;

- create a climate which enables other staff to develop and maintain positive attitudes towards the subject and confidence in teaching it.

Features of effective staff development

Leading and arranging staff development is an essential part of the role of the subject leader. It allows you to probe and challenge teachers' beliefs and practices, and to promote what you feel is effective teaching and learning.

There are expectations that a mathematics subject leader will make changes, raise standards and reach ambitious targets. These expectations may come from the head teacher, staff, governors and from you. Conducting an ongoing audit of the teaching of mathematics will allow you to identify specific issues which have an impact on the teaching and learning of mathematics. This is a powerful position. You are then able to publicise successes to the staff, head teachers and governors, and to address areas for development through staff development. The overall aim of staff development is to reach a shared understanding of mathematics and the features of effective teaching and learning of mathematics. Further reading on the role of the subject leader in sharing their own vision and implementing change can be found in Field (2000).

Staff development does not have to be formal. Informal discussions, demonstrations of ideas and staff room talk can be very effective ways of influencing teaching and learning. For example, you may notice that a teacher in the staff room talks about teaching children to add a zero when they multiply by ten. Knowing that this method can cause misconceptions which become evident when multiplying decimal fractions by ten, you might speak privately to that member of staff. You might demonstrate how the misconception might arise, and give a selection of examples of teaching strategies which avoid the error.

Therefore, it is possible to use many forms of staff development, some more formal than others. The following list is not exhaustive, but shows some of the possible types and forms of staff development. Just as in the classroom, your role is to make use of varied and appropriate strategies.

- Sending one or more members of staff for specific training sessions, and arranging their input to the rest of the staff during a meeting.

  The training is focused on key members of staff such as the teachers of Year 6 or the Foundation Stage. It may not always be appropriate for the training to be shared with all the staff, although it is usually good practice for all staff to have some insight into changes and developments taking place throughout the school, even if these do not directly concern them. This form of staff development is often called the cascade model. Transferring training amongst the staff in this way can be less effective than training everyone, but the teachers who attended the training themselves feel ownership of the ideas and changes they pass on to the rest of the staff.

- Feeding back to the rest of staff after attending training sessions yourself.

  Your own training is essential and it is important that you are confident in the role of advising colleagues. Often you are in a position to deliver the input in a more effective way, given your insight into the current practices of teaching and learning of mathematics.

- Staff meetings.

  This is a very effective method of staff development when several members of staff share a specific need, or the staff as a whole need to address an issue highlighted by your audit. However, staff meeting time is precious and limited, and you may need to use the information you have collected through your audit to convince your head teacher to allocate time to discuss mathematics. Staff meetings may of course take the form of workshops, discussions or dissemination of information. Whole school staff development is an important forum for the discussion of issues and for you to begin to share your vision of effective teaching of mathematics. Try to include governors, LSAs and supply teachers when at all possible to establish shared understanding of issues amongst all the people involved with mathematics.

- INSET days.

  These give the opportunity for extended sessions, and may also include input for supply teachers, LSAs and governors. Again, an important role of the subject leader is to convince the head teacher that training days should be devoted to mathematics. Your ability to do this may well depend on the sort of subject audit you have conducted and your subject development plan. However, there will still be times when other areas of the curriculum are a focus for whole school development, and mathematics is lower on the list of priorities. During these periods, less formal forms of staff development can be utilised.

- Consortium groups.

  Subject leaders of small schools which are geographically close to each other, or similar in needs, can usefully join together to provide staff development. Subject leaders can also support each other during regular meetings.

- Outside speakers.

  When a specific issue needs to be addressed you may feel that input from someone with previous relevant experience or knowledge will be effective. This might be for example an LEA advisor, a researcher, an NNS consultant or a teacher from another school. This option can be expensive, and requires careful liaison to ensure that the input is exactly what the school requires. An outside speaker, however, can provide the impetus to initiate a significant change. Again this may be an option for a consortium of schools to share the expense of a speaker who will meet a common need.

- Working with colleagues in the classroom.
  This can be a very effective method of focusing on important and real issues relating to teaching and learning, but, as discussed above, relies on an open relationship between classroom teacher and subject leader. These issues will be discussed in a later chapter.

Reflection

What are the features of effective staff development? (You might find it useful to reflect on your own experience of formal staff development, such as INSET days or courses.)

What makes a good professional development session?

- *A pace which is brisk, but at times allows reflection?*
- *Good quality information, imparted in an efficient manner?*
- *Chances to talk with colleagues or teachers from other schools?*
- *Handouts, overhead transparencies (OHTs) and activities which are appropriate?*
- *The appropriate tone of the course?*
- *What should be the balance between the dissemination of information, theoretical ideas, research findings, and practical ideas for the classroom?*

Identifying your own set of criteria for effective staff development can help you to assess your impact as a subject leader.

Providing staff development inevitably makes the subject leader aware of a tension between the development needs of individual teachers and the school as a whole. When collecting audit information, the subject leader will become aware of both sets of needs, which should have equal value if each teacher is to develop professionally. However, resources in the primary school are often limited. For example, you may find that one class teacher asks to attend several courses to develop their own interests and career pathway. The subject leader needs to discuss these issues thoroughly with the head teacher, who provides an overview of both school and individual needs.

Using the NNS Professional Development Materials

The NNS has produced a range of Professional Development Materials designed to be used by the subject leader to introduce and sustain changes in the teaching of mathematics. Many of these materials should be in each school and can also be found on the NNS website (www.standards.dfes.gov.uk/numeracy/).

These materials can be used to address ongoing issues for staff development. For example, there are materials to support you in using ICT to enhance teaching and learning in mathematics, or to lead workshops on the analysis of children's errors to assess their understanding. The materials are similar in some ways to a published scheme which is written for use with a class of children. The writers have some idea of the needs of an average child, but have no way of addressing individual needs of any child in a particular class. Assessment informs the provision of effective staff development. The collecting of audit information, even if this is very informal, allows the subject leader to base staff development on the achievements, strengths and needs of the school itself.

The materials are designed to be used flexibly, whether during a staff meeting, a whole school INSET session, or for individual teachers' self study. Certainly, some of the session ideas are suitable for all members of staff, including LSAs and the head; others may be suitable for just a few members of staff.

A critical approach, which matches the materials to the school's stage of development, is essential. For example, the materials include many OHTs. A subject leader who used every OHT included for each session would find that there are repetitions, and that the staff soon grow tired of this approach. Variety in the style of staff development is just as important as variety in teaching style in the classroom. OHTs can provide starting points for discussion and relevant information such as the NNS approach to the use of calculators. However, successful staff development is about establishing a shared understanding of the features of effective teaching and learning of mathematics. Therefore, it is important that the staff feel able to contribute their ideas, discuss thorny issues, and analyse their current practice. Time for open and honest discussion is essential. The use of official OHTs can remove the sense of ownership from the staff as a whole. Sometimes it is better for you to record ideas and summarise discussions yourself, and then perhaps include these in a rewording of the policy statement for mathematics.

The Professional Development Materials also include video footage of lessons. These should not necessarily be used as exemplars of good practice, but as stimulus for discussion. Members of staff may well be intimidated by footage showing practice which differs greatly from their own, and the purpose of using the video should be made clear before it is shown. Some videos include materials which can be used as a resource for the classroom such as NNS Video for Professional Development, Book 3, clip 5 on reflections, translations and rotations.

Effective use of NNS Professional Development Materials therefore relies on a sound knowledge of the current practice within the whole school, and a critical approach to the materials themselves. Where they do not serve the aims of the staff development, the materials should not be used, or should be extended with other readings, research findings or activities identified by the subject leader. The aims of the session should relate to the development plan for mathematics, and should be discussed with the head teacher. Where the staff development forms part of a staff meeting or INSET day, a clear agenda can provide a purpose for the day. Although of course flexibility is important, the subject leader may begin the session by stating its purpose.

For example, the session may aim to establish a shared understanding of the use of calculators in the curriculum, and this will result in an insertion of a relevant paragraph into the mathematics policy. Or the session may address the moderation of children's work against key objectives, which will result in a clear written procedure for reaching summative assessments at the end of each year. Accurate minutes will enable this purpose to be met, and also help to value staff contributions, and clarify further actions to be taken. A purpose can help to provide structure, but should not limit discussion of issues as they arise. Effective staff development often occurs when the staff themselves feel that the purpose of the session is useful and relevant. The subject leader will have to judge when the discussion has moved too far away from the central purpose, and when in fact the discussion, although it addresses other issues, is valuable in itself.

The subject audit may include gathering information from teachers as to the sorts of staff development they feel would have an impact on their teaching and understanding of mathematics. Similarly, asking the staff to evaluate staff development honestly and critically, as to content and style, can be useful.

The NNS Professional Development Materials include a selection of short and relevant articles as appendices, providing a feel for the literature published at the time of writing. These are extremely useful for the subject leader's role in maintaining knowledge of current issues. They may also be used as extra reading for other members of staff in order to sustain professional development, and to ensure changes in beliefs are more than skin deep.

Reflection

Reflect on a staff development session you have attended which has been based on NNS or National Literacy Strategy (NLS) Professional Development Materials. Draw up criteria for your own use of the materials.

Summary

There tend to be very few opportunities for formal staff development and so these should be used wisely. Your planning for these opportunities should be based on information gathered during your ongoing audit of current practices, and the changes you hope to promote. These may stem from your own beliefs and vision, and the expectations and requirements of government initiatives.

There can be many opportunities for effective informal staff development. Your relationships with your colleagues, however, should not be dominated by your desire to monitor their teaching and to implement developments. Your role will be to work with staff in an open way, just as you would want to gain support from any other subject leader. The staff of a primary school are a team, and working together will ensure that standards are raised.

3 WHOLE SCHOOL PLANNING

→ The National Standards for Subject Leadership state that subject leaders should:

- set expectations and targets for staff and pupils in relation to standards of pupil achievement and the quality of teaching;
- establish, with the involvement of relevant staff, short-, medium- and long-term plans for the development and resourcing of the subject which:
  - contribute to whole school aims, policies and practices including those in relation to behaviour, discipline, bullying and racial harassment;
  - are based on a range of comparative information and evidence, including the attainment of pupils;
  - identify realistic and challenging targets for improvement;
  - are understood by all those involved in putting the plans into practice;
  - are clear about action to be taken, timescales and criteria for success.

The subject leader is responsible for the teaching and learning of mathematics throughout the school, and is held accountable by colleagues, the head teacher, governors and OFSTED. However, the subject leader is rarely released from their own classroom for an extended period of time to fulfil this role, so planning at a whole school level is a realistic and useful way of influencing the teaching of colleagues.

Before the implementation of the NNS, the subject leader often produced a scheme of work or long-term plan which ensured coverage of the National Curriculum for mathematics, and provided continuity and progression. This complemented the policy statement for mathematics, and provided a more detailed basis for teachers' medium-term planning. It showed how the policy statement was put into practice. For example, it would often show how, in each year group, ICT was implemented into the curriculum for mathematics, how a progression of teaching in using and applying mathematics took place, and how mathematical vocabulary was systematically introduced.

The NNS now provides a long-term plan for Key Stages 1 and 2, with the *Curriculum Guidance for the Foundation Stage* providing a framework for teaching in the Early Years. However, many aspects of the curriculum are not covered by this plan, and the subject leader will want to ensure that these are discussed and a shared understanding is established. The results of discussion can be recorded in a whole school scheme of work, or can be monitored through a scrutiny of teachers' medium-term or weekly plans.

The advantage of writing a whole school scheme of work is that you can ensure progression and a coherent approach. The writing or review of such a scheme offers an ideal forum for discussing the issues, and is particularly useful in guiding newly appointed members of staff. However, schemes of work can be quite different from the reality of the classroom, and whole school planning which is drawn up by the subject leader, but is rarely referred to, can have little effect. The advantage of teachers' planning is that this should reflect reality more closely. Therefore monitoring whole school planning through teachers' medium-term and weekly plans can be a less formal approach and can be just as successful where you have an input into staff development and you can establish dialogue on key issues.

Ideally the subject leader could use both sorts of documentation – whole school planning in a written scheme of work, and teachers' medium-term and weekly planning – to ensure effective teaching and learning of mathematics. However, you will choose, in consultation with your staff, which one is best for your school.

The following areas can be used as subjects for sections of a whole school plan, or can be monitored through class teachers' planning, and discussed in staff development sessions:

1. progression and continuity from the Early Years throughout the primary school;
2. smooth transitions between year groups and Key Stages;
3. a whole school calculation strategy;
4. the effective use of published schemes;
5. the effective use of mathematical resources;
6. coherence in the teaching of using and applying mathematics (see Chapter 4 for more on this).

Mathematics in the Early Years

The subject leader of a primary or infant school needs to ensure that teachers of young children lay secure foundations for the later learning of mathematics, and successfully use the guidance provided for the Foundation Stage alongside the NNS framework. There has been much research relating to the way in which young children learn mathematics which can inform teaching. It is essential that you as the subject leader, particularly if you generally work in Key Stage 2, gain knowledge and if possible experience of mathematics in the Early Years. Until recently the early development of number had been strongly influenced by Piagetian theories and the importance of pre-counting skills such as matching and sorting. These have now been replaced in most cases by a belief in the central importance of children's counting skills. A full discussion of these areas can be found in Thompson (1997), Montague Smith (1997) and Pound (1999).

Some commercially published schemes still rely on the pre-counting skills of matching and sorting. The subject leader should be aware of the resources being used with nursery and Reception classes, and perhaps lead a discussion of research which lies behind certain approaches. For example, the research of Hughes (1986) reveals the considerable ability of children to use mathematics to solve problems when these are presented in a context which is meaningful. He showed that children are able to initiate and use their own conventions for written numerals, given a real context to do so. It is important therefore not to underestimate the learning young children bring to school and to present mathematical ideas in contexts which are meaningful.

Reflection

What are the beliefs of the teachers of Early Years in your school?

How closely are teachers able to work with parents and play groups to ensure they are aware of the knowledge and understanding that children bring to school?

Some teachers may need support in understanding how the requirements of the Foundation Stage and the NNS may be dovetailed together, particularly within a mixed class of Reception, Year 1 and perhaps Year 2. The Foundation Stage speaks of children learning through child initiated and structured play, and being allowed time to complete activities. Activities are not necessarily limited by fixed learning objectives, recognising a need to react flexibly to learning as it arises. However, some teachers interpret the requirements of the NNS as being much more formal, with a set structure to the lesson, which is naturally limited in time, and which works from clear learning objectives. The NNS does offer clear advice as to its implementation in the Reception Year, which can be found in Section 1 of the strategy and within the *Guide for your Professional Development* Book 4 (DfES). Further information can be found in the NNS *Mathematical Activities for the Foundation Stage.*

However, teachers may need support to incorporate play into lessons, and to experiment with models of the lesson. For example, a Reception lesson might start with a short whole class session on number rhymes, leading to group work that may include play activities, and that may take place at the same time or as part of a series of activities, with the plenary at a later stage of the day. A class catering for Reception, Year 1 and perhaps Year 2 children may adopt a more flexible approach. The class may work as a whole for a short time on number rhymes and mental and oral work, with either the younger or older children then being sent to work on an activity which may be in the role play area, whilst teaching input is given to the other group. Input may be given to the first group later in the lesson, ending with separate or whole class plenaries. You should be aware of and be able to justify the flexible models of lessons adopted by the Early Years class teacher.

Towards the end of the Reception Year, a more formal approach can be adopted when and if it is appropriate for the children concerned. It is important that staff work together in deciding a suitable approach so that each teacher is aware of the needs of their new classes. At the beginning of the year, teachers of Year 1 may need to continue with the progression towards a formal numeracy lesson if children have not been ready for this by the end of the Reception Year.

Transition between Year Groups and Key Stages

The subject leader of mathematics is responsible for the smooth transition between year groups and Key Stages, particularly when this involves a change of school. This role may involve evaluating the sorts of information which pass between teachers and schools.

Reflection

Which sort of information has been most useful to you when preparing to teach mathematics in September to a new class?

What are the views of your staff?

Information might include:

- test data and teacher assessments against National Curriculum levels and Early Learning Goals (certainly at the end of each Key Stage);

- assessments against NNS key objectives (certainly at the end of each year);

- information about children's work habits, their attitude to mathematics, their social development;

- levels of parental support and experiences of homework;

- children's self assessment of their learning;

- a sample of work;

- annotated medium-term plans from the previous year.

Team teaching can be an effective method of ensuring smooth transitions between schools. For example, if it is at all possible, an invitation to a Year 7 mathematics teacher to take a single lesson or series of lessons with Year 6 children can provide reassurance to the children themselves and an insight for both teachers. This can also take place within the same school, to prepare children for a change of teacher. The experience provides an opportunity for teachers to talk together and reinforce shared understandings of the nature of mathematics.

Managing transitions is about planning as well as assessment and record keeping. As subject leader you are responsible for progression and continuity between year groups. A whole school scheme of work or teachers' medium-term planning should hold up to a scrutiny which monitors coherence in the following areas.

Continuity and progression

Are class teachers fully aware of the expectations and experiences of children in the year below and above their own year group? This is particularly important at the beginning and end of a Key Stage. For example, are Key Stage I teachers fully aware of the way in which the NNS interacts with the *Guidance for the Foundation Stage*? Do Key Stage 2 teachers take the Key Stage 3 curriculum into account in their planning? If this an area for development, it might be useful for staff to track one area of mathematics such as the teaching of place value or 3D shape through the Foundation Stage, the NNS framework for Key Stage I and 2 and into Key Stage 3 to see the stages in progression.

Mathematical language

A natural extension of the above point is to scrutinise the use of mathematical vocabulary. Is vocabulary introduced in a systematic but meaningful way? Are terms used accurately, and are children given opportunities to use vocabulary and to negotiate its meaning? Do teachers have the secure subject knowledge necessary in order to introduce vocabulary in such a way as to ensure firm foundations for later learning? For example, if children are introduced to purely regular pentagons in the early years, they will have to renegotiate the definition of a pentagon when they are presented with irregular pentagons at a later stage.

ICT

Does the scheme of work, or teachers' medium-term planning, include coherent links to ICT to enhance teaching and learning? Is a range of ICT used systematically? Does progression in mathematics and ICT match progression in the ICT scheme of work? (There is a fuller discussion on this in Chapter 7.)

Bridging units

Do Year 6 teachers make use of the QCA bridging units in their planning to provide smooth transitions between Years 6 and 7? These can be ordered through the QCA website (www.qca.org.uk) and there are also transition units available from www.standards.dfes.gov.uk/numeracy/publications.

A clear calculation strategy

A scheme of work or medium-term planning should be underpinned by a clear calculation strategy which leads to children's effective and efficient use of mental, part-written, written and standard methods. This is an important area which will be discussed in more detail below.

A whole school calculation strategy

It is essential that the subject leader and the staff have a shared understanding of the policy of the NNS on calculation. This is an area which has undergone most change with the implementation of the NNS. You will need to be fully aware of the relevant issues and research findings which can be found in many texts but particularly in *Teaching Mental Calculation Strategies* (QCA, 1999), *Teaching Written Calculations* (QCA, 1999) and Thompson (1999).

There are also relevant sections in the NNS Professional Development Materials which can be used to lead staff development or for the subject leader's self study.

Ideally, following staff development in this area, there should be:

- a clear summary of the school's approach to calculation in the policy statement for mathematics;

- a full and detailed description of the calculation strategies taught in each year group in the whole school scheme of work and/or in each teacher's medium-term and weekly planning.

Reflection

Reflect on the current situation in school. If an OFSTED inspector were to question you as the subject leader and scrutinise documentation, would the school's approach to calculation be clear? If lessons were observed, would practice match this policy? For example, are mental strategies which are effective and appropriate for each year group directly taught to children? Are all teachers clear about the use of the Empty Number Line? Do all teachers know which compact standard methods are taught in Years 5 and 6, and do the methods taught in Years 3 and 4, and earlier, prepare for these standard methods? For example if you teach the decomposition method of subtraction in Years 5 and 6, then a strong understanding of partitioning of numbers should be developed throughout the school. If you decide to focus on complementary addition, then although partitioning is still important, there should be a focus on counting on and back in steps of 10, 50 100 etc from the Early Years onwards.

This sort of reflection is useful for any area of the curriculum, but particularly in the area of calculation as the NNS proposes an interaction between mental, part-written, written and standard methods which is quite different to previous practice.

For example, the NNS requires children to be taught a range of mental strategies, which should gradually be refined so that they become increasingly effective and efficient. Throughout the primary curriculum, children should attempt to solve problems mentally first, resorting to other methods when necessary. Calculations can be written down for several reasons. There may be too many steps or numbers to commit to memory, in which case jottings may be used to store information. These can be called part-written calculations. Mental calculations may be written down to describe mental strategies, using a model such as the Empty Number Line. This enables effective and efficient strategies to be demonstrated, and for assessment to take place. As children encounter problems with larger numbers and more complex calculations, the need to record becomes greater. However, written calculations can reflect mental calculations as much as possible, ensuring understanding at each stage. Written calculations are then refined so that they begin to match the highly efficient, compact and abbreviated standard methods.

What are the implications of these issues for formulating a whole school policy?

- Staff need to trust that children will, by the end of Key Stage 2, be introduced to at least one standard method in each of the four operations. In the past standard methods such as decomposition have been introduced as early as Year 2. A whole school approach can safeguard against early introduction to standard methods which often leads to misconceptions and rote learning of procedures.

- There needs to be a shared understanding of effective and efficient mental strategies appropriate for each year group. The QCA document *Teaching Mental Calculation Strategies* can help in this area, but staff may need time to try and discuss the strategies themselves. Effective strategies need to reflect the individual problem itself. For example, when tackling 17 + 14, a partitioning or bridging method may be effective whereas 16 + 17 may be best calculated as a near double. The subject leader will need to take a lead in formulating a shared understanding of the terms for and the characteristics of flexible mental strategies.

- Models such as the Empty Number Line can be explored as a means of supporting mental strategies, making these strategies clear to other children as teaching points and to allow assessment. Staff development may call upon research findings from the Netherlands on the Empty Number Line, which can be found in Thompson (1999) and Anghileri (2001).

- A whole school approach to modelling the recording of written calculations will ensure that this becomes a smooth process. For example, a child who describes a mental strategy of adding 16 and 7 as:

16 and 4 is 20 and then 3 more is 23

can be supported by the teacher in recording this on the Empty Number Line:

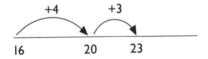

or as a series of number sentences:

16 + 4 = 20
20 + 3 = 23

However, you will need to ensure that the teacher does not model this in a mathematically incorrect way:

16 + 4 = 20 + 3 = 23
Clearly, 16 + 4 is not equal to 23

Each member of staff should model this sort of recording following the rule of a new line for each step. This can be shared with the children. A class teacher may need support in marking a child's mistake such as this. Although it is mathematically incorrect, it is an important step towards effective recording, so the teacher may not want to mark it wrong in a child's book. The staff may decide therefore on a policy of praising such a response, but adding a correct recording of the strategy next to the child's own.

- The school as a whole will also need to agree on the reasons for introducing compact standard methods at all, and which ones will be taught. If the teaching of calculations is seen as a gradual path towards these methods then every teacher should be aware of where the path will end. For example, you may decide that the teaching of long division is problematic as it is not easily explained to allow full understanding. The Dutch chunking method of repeated subtraction may therefore be taught in Years 5 and 6, in which case there should be an emphasis throughout the whole school on repeated subtraction.

- The school calculation policy may refer to the use of calculators. (See Chapter 7 for a full discussion on the use of ICT in mathematics.)

When the whole school approach to calculation is secure, it may be useful to inform parents of its key elements. This is an area where parents are likely to want to work with the school to support their children's learning, and again a consistent approach is essential. Some parents may need to be persuaded that the approach taken by the school is the most effective, and workshops can be very useful in exploring these ideas with parents. Research findings, found in the texts mentioned above, can be used to back up a presentation of the school's approach.

Effective use of published schemes

Some commercially published schemes attempt to provide whole school planning, even to the extent of detailed lesson plans. It has been emphasised so far that whole school planning should be based upon the subject leader's audit of the current provision within the school and plans for its development, and should be the product of staff discussions. It is unlikely therefore that a published scheme could offer exactly the most appropriate form of whole school planning for an individual school. However, a subject leader can use commercially published schemes as a resource for ideas.

There may be some pressure from individual teachers for the purchase of a published scheme to support the everyday teaching of mathematics. A purchase of this kind is a major expense and does not necessarily lead to the raising of standards. The following guidelines might be useful when evaluating schemes:

- Does the scheme fit with the staff's beliefs in the nature of mathematics?
- Is the scheme flexible?
- Are resources attractive?
- Are they easy to use?
- Do they offer appropriate mathematical activities?
- Do they refer to the National Curriculum, the NNS and the Early Learning Goals?

- How much photocopying is involved?
- What support is there for mental and oral work?
- Are teachers supported in direct, whole class, interactive teaching?
- What is the approach to recording?
- Is mathematical vocabulary introduced systematically?
- Are there ideas for problem solving and investigative activities?
- Are the resources required for practical activities easily available and inexpensive?
- If ideas for games are included are these ready made and hard wearing?
- Are ideas for differentiation manageable?
- Is a wide range of learners catered for?
- Are able children offered an enriched or accelerated curriculum?
- Do activities motivate all children, including boys and girls from a range of backgrounds with a variety of interests?
- Are there consumable workbooks? How will this expense be met each year?
- How is assessment tackled? Is it effective and efficient? Will it provide information to inform planning?
- Are the skills of using and applying mathematics assessed?
- Will the resources save teacher time or increase workload?
- Does the approach to mental and written calculations match the beliefs of the staff?
- Are there homework ideas?

Many subject leaders find that an over reliance on published schemes can limit the teaching and learning of mathematics. This was established by an OFSTED report, *The NNS: an Interim Evaluation by HMI* (2001).

The report stated that:

> 'Many teachers have found that by moving away from their reliance on published mathematics schemes, through which pupils worked at their own pace, and by following the year-by-year teaching programme set out clearly in the Framework, their expectations have been raised significantly.' pages 10 to 11

Ineffective use of a scheme is a difficult area to address, but can be the basis of staff development. Most teachers are happy to point out the negative aspects of their own published scheme. This can be a starting point for staff development. Over reliance on a published scheme can be due to:

- weak subject knowledge;
- a limited repertoire of ideas and activities;
- an uncertainty regarding the modification of activities to cater for a range of learners;
- a lack of time in which to undertake planning.

Staff development can be an effective way to identify and address the reasons for overuse. It can, for example, have an impact on subject knowledge, and can provide opportunities to share ideas for activities and strategies for differentiation. The published schemes may still be used in many cases as a bank of ideas, but guidelines can be agreed with the staff as to appropriate and critical use.

Effective use of mathematical resources

Whole school planning offers an opportunity to establish guidelines for the appropriate use of resources and may for example address:

- A shared understanding of the role of resources in supporting children's learning. For example, you might consider yourself and with your staff the purposes of resources in the mathematics lesson:

  Some resources allow children to build an understanding of concepts such as non-standard units of measurement

  Some resources are designed to scaffold children's learning, offering a physical model of mathematical concepts such as base 10 blocks, number squares, number lines and place value cards. The Empty Number Line could be seen as a model to scaffold children's learning of calculations.

  Some resources are used to record mathematics such as digit cards and small white boards.

  Some resources offer opportunities for child initiated and structured play. These may include shops, post offices, travel agencies, and food outlets. Resources and time opportunities need to be planned for children to initiate their own play. A list of key vocabulary and questions situated next to the play area can allow a parent helper or other adult to structure the activity when it is appropriate.

- Details of which resources are used for each purpose, with some guidance for the use of particular resources for particular age ranges, although this may be flexible to cater for individual learners. For example, children in Reception and Year 1 should use a number track to aid counting and counting on. This relates well to snakes and ladders type of board games. Children should progress to using number lines, as these are more mathematically accurate, showing that there may be other numbers lying between each whole number.

- Guidance on the way in which resources may avoid or contribute to misconceptions. For example money place value cards address the misconception that one pound and 6 pence is recorded £1.6. However, an activity involving multiplying a decimal fraction by 10 on a calculator can reinforce the misconception that the decimal point moves, rather than the digits.

- Health and safety guidance on, for example, the use of scissors, compasses, and ICT equipment.

Summary

Teachers are generally ready to take on the role of subject leader when they become aware of the experiences of children throughout the school. A newly qualified teacher focuses almost entirely on their own teaching and the needs of the children in their own classroom. A subject leader is aware of and cares about the learning of all the children in every class in the school. This overview is essential for monitoring progression and continuity, and providing information to report to OFSTED when necessary.

You may have very definite ideas about the teaching and learning of mathematics, and will want to promote these. This is an important role of the subject leader. However, during the process of discussing and producing whole school planning, you may find that the ideas and beliefs you hold need to be modified and negotiated in order to reach a shared understanding with the staff. Consistency is important, and you may well have to compromise. Having an impact on the beliefs of staff takes time. When you work with staff who initially hold very different beliefs to yours, whole school planning can be part of the gradual implementation of change.

4 USING AND APPLYING MATHEMATICS

The National Standards for Subject Leadership state that subject leaders should:

- set expectations and targets for staff and pupils in relation to standards of pupil achievement and the quality of teaching;
- ensure curriculum coverage, continuity and progression in the subject for all pupils, including those of high ability and those with special educational or linguistic needs;
- provide guidance on the choice of appropriate teaching and learning methods to meet the needs of the subject and of different pupils.

The skills of using and applying mathematics are detailed in the National Curriculum Attainment Target 1 (MA1) in the areas of problem solving, communicating and reasoning, where specific skills are detailed for each Key Stage. The skills of using and applying mathematics are at least as essential as the content specified in Attainment Targets 2,3 and 4. The content of mathematics is often forgotten when not used in everyday life, but the skills of problem solving, the ability to estimate and hypothesise, and the confidence to tackle unknown situations in mathematics are fundamental. The DfES report in 1999, *From Thinking Skills to Thinking Classrooms*, certainly emphasises the importance of these skills, which many teachers feel are an essential part of the curriculum.

The NNS provides great detail on the content of mathematics lessons for each year in the form of detailed objectives in section 3 of the Framework. However, it provides less guidance as to how MA1 should be tackled and broken down for each year group. For example, the NNS states as an identical objective for each of Years 4, 5 and 6:

> 'Solve mathematical problems or puzzles, recognise and explain patterns and relationships, generalise and predict. Suggest extensions asking "What if?"'
> (NNS *Framework for Teaching Mathematics from Reception to Year 6*, Section 3 pages 19, 23, 27)

Although examples of activities are given in the NNS Supplement of Examples Sections 5 and 6, there is no clear idea of progression in this area, as there is for example in the teaching of mental strategies for addition and subtraction.

Therefore, the subject leader will need to ensure that the skills of using and applying mathematics are taught systematically and coherently throughout the school. Whole school planning documents and staff development can provide guidance and support.

Staff development should include LSAs and governors to ensure a shared understanding of issues amongst as many people as possible.

Providing staff development on using and applying mathematics

An important starting point would be to establish, through written planning and more preferably staff discussion, shared definitions of the two main areas where the skills of using and applying are best focused: problem solving and investigative work.

Problem solving

Usually, problem solving questions describe a situation which needs some sort of solution and are usually phrased as closed questions such as:

> How many teams of 4 can we make from our class of 30?
> What is the smallest number of coins we can use to pay the shopping bill of £2.71?

The NNS states that problems set for children should be relevant to their lives. However, classroom activities are rather different to the lives of most children, and indeed some of the examples given by the NNS as 'real life problems', are clearly not so, for example:

> There are 2 red buttons and 4 blue buttons on a card of buttons. How many buttons are there on 10 cards?

> (from NNS *Framework*, Section 5 page 67)

Skills which can be taught or consolidated through problem solving include:

- estimation, hypothesising and checking answers to see if they are reasonable for the given problem;
- breaking down a complex problem into simpler steps, for example identifying steps within two-step problems such as:

> What change would you have from £1 after buying a newspaper for 45p and a can of Coke for 32p?

These skills need to be taught directly; children do not always acquire them naturally.

Investigations

When using investigations, situations are described which the children are encouraged to explore, usually including an open question to investigate, for example:

> Which totals can be made by adding consecutive numbers?

Some investigations begin with a closed question and encourage children to ask their own open 'What if' questions. For example:

> If 5 people in a room shake hands with each other, how many handshakes will take place? How many handshakes take place with other numbers of people? Can you spot a pattern? Can you predict how many handshakes for any number of people in a room?

Some investigative activities attempt to relate to real life such as:

> After Christmas, a post office is left with only a supply of 3p and 5p stamps. Which amounts can be made by using these stamps?

Many investigations explore mathematics itself:

> When you add two even numbers together, what sorts of totals do you make?

The skills that can be taught or consolidated through investigations include:

- organising and refining ways of recording. For example, when generating patterns in the handshake investigation, children may explore and evaluate diagrammatical methods of recording the handshakes, and tabulate results showing the number of handshakes for each total number of people;

- searching for pattern in their results. For example children may generate several examples of addition number sentences using only even numbers. They can then be taught to reflect on the totals made, and note similarities among their results, leading to the generalisation that they are all even numbers;

- understanding and investigating general statements. For example, children might generate examples to test the statement 'All multiples of 6 are also multiples of 2 and 3'. Or the teacher might want to explore possible reasons for general statements. For example, children may use pairs of socks or multilink towers in groups of two to explain why adding odd and even numbers give odd totals. Children can also investigate statements which are not true such as 'All pentagons do not tessellate'.

- some investigational activities introduce children to the idea of proof. For example, when children list all the combinations possible when two ordinary dice are thrown, this could be seen as an example of proof by exhaustion, a recognised method of proof. Discussing why two odd numbers added together result in an even number in more general terms, rather than relying on a number of examples, also introduces the idea of proof being a convincing argument. Teachers in Year 6 can make use of the QCA *Bridging Units in Mathematics: Algebra* (2002), and all staff should have an understanding of the ways in which mathematics in Key Stages 1 and 2 lays foundations for future learning of algebra as described in NNS *Framework for Teaching Mathematics*, Section 1, pages 9–10.

Again these skills often need to be identified by class teachers, and modelled and evaluated within lessons.

It is interesting to note the use of the term puzzle in the NNS as a third focus for work on using and applying mathematics. For example, each year group has as an objective in the yearly programme: 'solve mathematical problems or puzzles'. A puzzle may be included as a problem-solving activity as it makes use of a closed question such as:

> Arrange the numbers 1, 2, 3 ... to 9 in the circles so that each side of the square adds up to 12.

(from NNS Framework, Section 6, page 78)

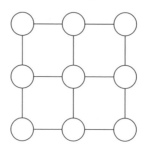

A puzzle may also lend itself to an open question often investigating an aspect of mathematics itself, and therefore could be classified as an investigation:

> Put 1, 2 or 3 in each circle so that each side adds up to 5. You can use each number as often as you like. Find different ways of doing it.

(from NNS Framework, Section 5, page 62)

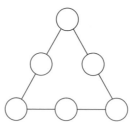

The use of puzzles might be an area for staff discussion.

Staff development sessions may then involve the staff as a whole undertaking a problem solving or investigational activity. Engaging in mathematics as a learner is an important process in reflecting on the teaching of skills of using and applying mathematics. The staff can then be led to reflect on the confidence required to tackle these activities and the skills used to complete them. These skills can be compared with those listed in the National Curriculum MA1 in order to reach a common definition of each, and a shared understanding of their importance. It may be useful to use the description of Using and Applying skills within the Programmes of Study for MA 2, 3 and 4 rather than just the level descriptors for MA1.

Members of staff may not necessarily remember being taught these skills directly. It is interesting to gather views on whether these skills need to be taught. Some children, for example, appear to be able to generalise and break problems down into manageable steps; others need direct input in these areas. The three-part numeracy lesson offers opportunities for children to practise skills during the mental and oral work. Direct modelling of problem solving and investigative skills can take place during the teaching input. Children can then undertake activities in pairs, groups or individually during the main part of the lesson. The plenary acts as an opportunity to describe and reflect upon strategies used to complete activities. Evaluation of strategies is an important part of refinement towards increasingly effective and efficient methods. This may take place over two or more lessons as investigations in particular can, and should, be extended.

Staff can be invited to bring to the session their favourite problem solving and investigative activities. Teachers often have a bank of activities they enjoy using, which can in some cases lead to children repeating the same activity during their time at the school, and never being introduced to certain skills. The skills of using and applying embedded in these favourite activities can then be categorised by the staff. (Many activities will involve more than one specific skill listed in MAI, but will probably focus more on one than others.) This can be drawn up into a flexible whole school plan which gives some idea of the skills to be taught and the activities that can be used with each year group. You may find that there are some omissions, for example there may be no activities currently used within the school that allow children to investigate general statements, in which case the subject leader can suggest appropriate activities for each year group.

Whole school planning in terms of using and applying can never be as tightly documented as other areas. The relevant skills are not taught in one year group alone, they need to be consolidated using increasingly complex situations. Similar activities may need to be repeated to allow children to consolidate skills. For example, children in Year 2 may be set the challenge of finding out how many different outfits a clown could make from two different coloured noses and two different coloured hats. Further noses and hats may be added, and then a selection of bow ties.

> Billy the Clown has two party noses, one red and one white, and two hats, one plain and one patterned.
>
> How many different outfits can he make?
>
> He buys two bowties, one spotted and one striped. How many outfits can he make now?

This investigation can be used to teach children to explore combinations, to record their results systematically, and to make predictions and conjectures. Further activities will be necessary to consolidate these skills. For example children can then find the number of combinations of scoops of ice creams of two different flavours, with two types of cone, and with choices of two sauces.

> How many different ice creams can you make with two sorts of ice cream, chocolate and strawberry, and two types of cones, plain and chocolate?
>
> You are allowed one scoop of ice cream and one cone.
>
> If you are allowed to pour one type of sauce on top, either strawberry or toffee, how many different ice creams could you make now?

Repetition of similar activities allows identification of specific skills, and provides children with opportunities to reflect on strategies. Older children may be reintroduced to the clown and ice cream activities in order that they may start to construct general statements about the relationship between the number of elements to be combined and the number of combinations. For example, 2 noses x 2 hats = 4 outfits; 2 noses x 2 hats x 2 bowties = 8 outfits.

So activities can be purposefully repeated, but teachers should be clear as to which skills of using and applying mathematics can be taught or consolidated through each activity.

The subject leader should have an overview of progression in each of the elements of MAI. For example, children in Years 1 and 2 may investigate general statements about adding odd and even numbers, or the effect on the units digit of adding ten to a number; in Years 3 and 4 they might discuss general statements such as all the common multiples of 2 and 5 are multiples of 10, any odd number is one more than a double; Years 5 and 6 children may investigate general statements relating to the internal angles of 2D shapes and construct their own general statements.

It can be more difficult to assess the skills of MAI as they tend to be spoken or thought rather than recorded through writing. Once the staff as a whole has discussed these skills it will be easier for teachers to assess and record progress when working with a focus group. Teachers of young children may need to assess MAI through working with small groups, rotating around the class. Older children can be encouraged to record thoughts, ideas, predictions and conjectures in thought bubbles in their written work. It is my experience that children enjoy annotating their work with thought bubbles, perhaps because it is associated with comic type literature. Given the reassurance that thinkers can always change their minds, children can feel secure enough to record thoughts without fear of failure. This process will need to be modelled by the teacher.

Summary

Using a whole school scheme of work or planning document, staff development sessions and a scrutiny of teachers' planning, the subject leader needs to be confident that:

- the staff have a shared understanding of the skills of using and applying mathematics and of their importance;
- these skills are taught directly to children;
- there is some progression and continuity in the teaching of these skills;
- each skill detailed in the National Curriculum for Mathematics is taught and the activities used are broad and balanced;
- activities are not repeated unnecessarily but are used purposefully;

- assessment of the skills detailed in the National Curriculum takes place and these records passed on to future teachers.

It may be useful for you to read Thompson (1999), which describes the Dutch use of problems in the teaching of mathematics which is significantly different to practice in England. Hughes et al (2000) is a useful discussion of research relating to using and applying mathematics.

5 MEETING INDIVIDUAL CHILDREN'S NEEDS AND CO-ORDINATING THE INCLUSIVE TEACHING OF MATHEMATICS

(→) The National Standards for Subject Leadership state that subject leaders should:

- work with the SENCO (Special Educational Needs co-ordinator) and any other staff with Special Educational Needs (SEN) expertise, to ensure that individual education plans are used to set subject specific targets and match work well to pupils' needs;
- establish clear targets for pupils' achievement, and evaluate progress and achievement by all pupils, including those with special educational linguistic needs;
- ensure curriculum coverage, continuity and progression in the subject for all pupils, including those of high ability and those with special educational or linguistic needs;
- use data effectively to identify pupils who are underachieving and, where necessary, create and implement effective plans of action to support those pupils;
- provide guidance on the choice of appropriate teaching and learning methods to meet the needs of the subject and of different pupils;
- deploy, or advise the head teacher on the deployment of, staff involved in working with pupils with SEN to ensure the most efficient use of teaching and other expertise.

This chapter will address the role of the subject leader in ensuring inclusive practices within the teaching of mathematics, addressing the teaching of able children, children with specific learning difficulties and the implementation of Booster and Springboard programmes.

The subject leader must be prepared to read and share with their staff new developments and thinking in inclusive policies. Part of the subject leader's role is to evaluate continually current provision throughout the school against research findings and educational literature. That is not to say that every new initiative and change of policy should be implemented in a blind way. A critical and discerning approach is essential.

Reflection

Are you aware of individual children in your school with additional mathematical needs or learning or behaviour needs which have an impact on their progress in mathematics? Do Individual Education Plans (IEP) in your school include targets which relate to mathematics?

Part of the initial and continuing audit of the teaching of mathematics will include a study of inclusion. For example as subject leader you will need to consider the following areas.

- Can specific needs be met within the whole class setting?
- Are individual children supported during whole class discussions?
- Are children withdrawn from classes?
- Which areas do they miss when they are withdrawn?
- Does the school's requirements for planning support teachers in meeting the needs of a range of ability?
- Is differentiation appropriate and manageable?
- How are parents involved?
- How are LSAs used to support children's learning?
- How do LSAs feel about the way they work?
- Are LSAs involved with planning?
- Are LSAs trained appropriately?
- Are there strategies to ensure children do not become over reliant on LSA support?
- How are able children identified and catered for within the school?
- Is it possible to consult the child's next school when addressing the needs of gifted and talented children?
- When children work on the Springboard or Booster programmes, are connections made between this work and their numeracy lessons?

The National Curriculum states 'schools have a responsibility to provide a broad and balanced curriculum for all pupils' and three principles for inclusion are described as:

- setting suitable learning challenges;
- responding to pupils' diverse learning needs;
- overcoming potential barriers to learning and assessment for individuals and groups of children.

(DfES/QCA, 1999, page 30)

After an initial audit, the three National Curriculum principles can be helpful in guiding your development of the inclusive teaching of mathematics.

Setting suitable learning challenges

This principle highlights the importance of teaching based on assessment. Your programme of staff development may need to establish clear procedures for the assessment of mathematics so that teachers can judge whether challenges are in fact suitable for individual children. High expectations are essential, and these can only be set when backed by sound assessments. Specialist diagnostic assessments may need to be available for use with individual children with specific difficulties such as tests for auditory memory.

Learning challenges can be short-term activities or objectives for day to day lessons, or could be seen as longer term targets. For example, a teacher may plan a unit of work for two weeks on mental strategies in addition, and set a challenge for children to meet by the end of the topic of work. Targets can help to focus teaching and learning. The NNS *Framework for Teaching Mathematics* highlights this in Section I, page 36. Targets can be set for whole classes, ability groups or individuals. Targets of course need to be carefully matched to individuals, based on sound assessments, so that they are SMART (specific, measurable, achievable, realistic and timed). Parents and children should be involved in identifying and negotiating the target, and targets should relate to the curriculum covered during that specific period of time. Activities can be set to support children and parents at home working towards the target. Setting an unrealistic target, or one which is not monitored or is divorced from the actual curriculum, can be detrimental.

Setting targets for groups or classes of children can never be as accurate as setting them for individuals. However, the negotiation and monitoring of individual targets for a class of children can be time-consuming so the subject leader needs to lead the staff in finding a compromise between the ideal and the realistic. The NNS provides guidance in this area in *Guide for your Professional Development* Book 4.

One model is to set group targets for the majority of the class, with a small number of individual children having their own targets, which relate to their own individual pro-grammes. For example, a Year 3 class may have groups working at three different levels, and the teacher may set targets for each group:

- to derive quickly doubles of all numbers to 20 with corresponding halves;
- to derive quickly doubles of 5 to 50 with corresponding halves;
- to derive quickly doubles of 5 to 100 with corresponding halves.

These may be targets for a half term during which the teacher and children model strategies for doubling, practise rapid recall of doubles during the mental and oral starter, and the children take doubling games home to play as homework. Of course, individual children may not fit into the three groups of ability. In these cases, individual targets, which may relate to IEPs or individual programmes, can be set:

- to know by heart all doubles of numbers to 5;
- to derive quickly doubles of multiples of 50 to 500.

The setting of targets in similar areas of mathematics allows the class to work together for a proportion of the numeracy lesson. A class with a smaller range of ability may have just one or two targets.

Class teachers will need to be sensitive about displaying differentiated targets in the classroom. Success should be celebrated, but the child who does not reach their target will need extra support and opportunities to meet it at a later stage. In these cases, it is important to monitor progress carefully during the set period of time so that possible difficulties are identified early and more appropriate targets set.

Ideally, targets should be incorporated in the medium-term planning as ongoing work, perhaps during mental and oral starters. You may be able to develop a system where staff annotate their medium-term planning with group and individual targets so these can be monitored by you and the SENCO. Therefore, target setting may be part of planning rather than an extra requirement for teachers. Record keeping systems need to be efficient and, in cases where these may be used to provide evidence of a need for increased support for individual children, comprehensive.

Responding to pupils' diverse learning needs

The NNS (DfES, 1999) states clearly that differentiation should be manageable, usually at no more than three levels of work on the same area of mathematics. However, this level of differentiation may not be sufficient to include all children and meet individual needs. For example, a class teacher may need support in meeting the needs of a particularly able child within a class, or a small group or children with specific difficulties. The subject leader can work alongside class teachers in formulating modified objectives for particular groups or individuals, which can be recorded on the medium-term planning for the class. These modified objectives would form a group education plan or IEP, and link to class, group and individual targets. Modified objectives can be taken from objectives listed in the NNS for earlier or later year groups.

Where children are working towards level I of the National Curriculum, the P levels can provide useful modified objectives. Information can be found in *Planning, Teaching and Assessing the Curriculum for Pupils with Learning Difficulties* (QCA, 2001) and *Towards the National Curriculum for Mathematics: Examples of what pupils with special educational needs should be able to do at each P level* (DfES, 2001).

One useful idea, suitable for a workshop-type staff meeting, is to consider the modification of activities to include a wide range of learners. This sort of discussion can lead to a shared understanding of manageable inclusive practices. For example, the subject leader might begin the session by showing one of the activities taken from the booklet *Reasoning about Numbers, with Challenges and Simplifications* which can be found at www.standards.dfes.gov.uk/numeracy/publications. This document suggests simple activities with ideas for extensions and modifications, such as the following:

Christmas Cards

Everyone in this room sends a Christmas card to everyone else. How many Christmas cards are sent?

Simplifications:
How many Christmas cards would there be for 3 people? 4 people? How many Christmas cards for the people on your table?

Challenges:
How many Christmas cards for 100 people?

Can you make up a rule to find out how many Christmas cards for any number of people?

This idea of children working at different levels of the same activity can lead to discussion of the inclusion of all children in whole class teaching. You can see this sort of discussion as an opportunity to share and reach a common understanding of effective teaching and learning of mathematics. The emphasis on whole class teaching in the NNS was in part a response to comparative studies of countries that appear to score highly on international tests and that make use of this teaching strategy. More information can be found at www.timss.bc.edu/

As a subject leader, it is important you discuss features of effective whole class teaching such as:

- high expectations for all children;
- brisk pace;
- direct and interactive teaching;
- varied use of resources;
- variety of activities;
- a range of open and closed questions supporting children at various levels of understanding;
- all children involved where possible;
- appropriate but discreet use of support staff;
- the use of mixed ability pairs of children to discuss ideas and methods, and answer questions in mental and oral work.

The inclusion of all children in whole class teaching is based on the belief that children will learn from each other. This belief has to be balanced with the needs of individual children, and the effect on the rest of the class of, for example, the inclusion of a child with severe behaviour or learning difficulties. Each case needs to be assessed individually.

The three part lesson, although focusing on whole class, direct, interactive teaching, does lend itself to a variety of methods of grouping children.

Reflection

Are you aware of the way in which teachers in your school group children within their classes? If you make use of setting by ability across classes, can you justify this if necessary to parents or an OFSTED inspector?

The benefits of each type of grouping can be a topic for discussion during staff development.

Whole class teaching

This allows the teacher to introduce new ideas, model skills, and promote discussion between children across the class. The calculating methods of more able children can be used as teaching points. However, it can be difficult to meet the needs of all the children effectively.

Ability groups

Setting suitable learning challenges is simplified by grouping the children by ability. Differentiation is more manageable, and the children interact with others of a similar ability who are tackling the same task. However, children who constantly work in an ability group begin to identify their mathematical potential with the level of group they are in. Teacher expectations may be too high or too low for individuals, and it may become difficult for children to move into higher groups if the gap between the groups becomes too wide. It may also be true that a child should be in a lower group for number work, but a higher one for shape and space, for example.

Ability pairs

A group of four children allows six separate channels of communication, which for confident children can be very beneficial. However, some children are intimidated by large groups. Carefully chosen ability pairs can provide a setting for more controlled and balanced interaction.

Mixed ability groups

Mixed ability groupings allow children to interact with a wider range of children, and can provide a refreshing change of context. Less able children learn from more able children, who in turn are required to discuss and explain, clarifying their own thoughts.

Mixed ability pairs

As above, pairing children can help prevent the dominance of one child over a group and can allow quieter children to play an active role.

Individual work

Individual work is best used only for assessment purposes, given the social nature of learning mathematics.

Setting children for mathematics

Some schools are responding to the challenges of delivering effective whole class teaching by setting children across year groups into ability teaching groups. This policy has the advantage of presenting the teacher with a small ability range, allowing more manageable differentiation.

The effects of setting on children's learning have not been fully researched at this time, but there are concerns about the possible movement of children between sets. A child who finds himself in the lower set at an early stage in their education, may not be able to move out of this set and into a higher one if, as the sets progress, the gaps between them become sgnificantly wider. Lower sets also miss the input of brighter children during whole class discussions. Although continual comparison with more able children can have a discouraging effect, a teacher can use a more able child to demonstrate and model effective strategies. Current research findings are discussed in Koshy (2001), and subject leaders may find it useful to be fully aware of the available data when leading discussions in this area.

When leading whole staff discussions which address the possible organisation of mathematics through sets, the subject leader might reflect on these issues:

- The organisation of sets needs to be fair and straightforward in order that it may be justified to children, parents, representatives of the LEA and OFSTED inspectors. Where the organisation makes use of test data, this should be supplemented by teacher assessment to provide a rounded assessment of each child.
- The allocation of teachers to sets needs careful consideration. Some sets may be more desirable than others. Less confident teachers who continually opt for lower ability sets may limit their own professional development. Clearly the teachers of able sets need secure subject knowledge, but it could be argued that every set requires a confident teacher, particularly the lower sets.
- The needs of able children may well be met through setting in that opportunities for either enrichment or acceleration may be available. For example, the setting of able children allows a group of children to follow enrichment activities together, enabling interaction to take place. Younger able children can be accelerated through sets to join older children. However, these children may still have their final year working on the next year's curriculum alone.
- It is possible in smaller schools that brothers and sisters may find themselves taught in the same set. The effect on both children should be considered, and parents consulted.
- Setting has implications for assessment, recording and reporting procedures, requiring teachers to work closely together. This may be a positive feature as it increases opportunities for professional dialogue, but could lead to an isolation of mathematics from other subjects. For example, what opportunities will there be for cross-curricular learning of mathematics? This will be an important issue if you are hoping to promote a connectionist belief in the teaching and learning of mathematics.
- Setting needs constant review. It is important that children are able to move from one set to another when appropriate. Therefore the sets should not be allowed to grow too separate, and some sort of catch up programme may be needed to allow movement between sets.

It is worth considering whether setting favours teaching rather than learning. Certainly the teacher's task is simplified, but opportunities for children to learn from each other, to discuss ideas and explain strategies may be limited. It is important that the staff reaches an honest and shared understanding of these issues, and can clearly justify the organisation of mathematics. This understanding should be reflected in the policy statement. Whichever decision is reached, to use setting or not, a flexible approach that constantly evaluates practice and allows the needs of individual children to be taken into account is essential.

Overcoming potential barriers to learning and assessment for individuals and groups of children

Reflection

Are there potential barriers for children's learning of mathematics? It is worth taking an honest look at your own teaching, and the teaching throughout the school. Possible barriers lie in:

- *low teacher expectations;*
- *teachers' insecure subject knowledge of mathematics or of styles of learning or of the needs of individual children;*
- *teachers' over-reliance on a particular teaching style;*
- *children's experiences of failure leading to low confidence;*
- *a curriculum which does not cater for children's auditory, visual or other physical difficulties which may be as common as left-handedness where scissors are not appropriate;*
- *a curriculum which does not cater for children's specific learning difficulties such as dyscalculia, dyslexia etc;*
- *a curriculum which is not accessible for children with English as an additional language.*

A very useful resource is the NNS document *Guidance to Support Pupils with Specific Needs in the Daily Mathematics Lesson* (DfES, 2001), available from www.standards. dfes.gov.uk/numeracy/publications. This file provides information on a range of needs and disorders and advice on how specific parts of the National Curriculum may need to be modified to ensure learning. However, all children's needs are individual and the file can only provide a starting point for teachers.

Addressing the learning of children with specific learning difficulties or with EAL requires a two-pronged approach.

- These difficulties can be seen as potential barriers for inclusion in to learning. Delivery of the curriculum may need to be modified to ensure access for all children. For example, activities may need to be presented in a visual form to children with English as an additional language. A child who has a poor auditory memory may need to have instructions given simply and regularly to enable participation in activities. In some cases resources can be used to minimise barriers, such as calculators, number squares, table squares etc. Therefore everyday activities may need to be evaluated and modified.
- Specific difficulties, however, still need to be addressed. For example, children with EAL may need to have additional opportunity to use and explore language with adult support. The child with limited auditory memory skills may benefit from short, specifically designed tasks which help to develop these skills.

Reflection

What is the current approach in your school? Do current practices cover both these aspects?

The subject leader, working with the SENCO, may need to advise on how both these aspects can be addressed. Often specialist advice is required and the subject leader acts as a liaison with outside agencies.

A further investigation of the school's inclusive practices can be undertaken using Booth et al (2000). The subject leaders, head teacher, SENCO and preferably the whole staff should work together in evaluating current practice.

Co-ordinating LSA support in the teaching of mathematics

Teaching assistant, classroom assistant or learning support assistant support is an expensive and important resource. LSAs (as a general term for any assistant) often have most contact with children whose learning and emotional needs do not easily fit into ability groups. Therefore it is worth considering whether they should be included in any staff development you provide which establishes a common under-standing of the nature of effective learning of mathematics.

For example, sessions where you discuss beliefs about mathematics and the use of mathematical language, or where you agree how resources should be used, can use-fully involve LSAs. Their views can be collected during your audits of mathematics, and their training needs considered. You may need to negotiate their access to plan-ning, bearing in mind that class teachers' planning and record keeping will address individual children and there are issues of confidentiality. The head teacher and SENCO usually establish guidelines for confidentiality, but you will need to be aware of these. For example, it may be appropriate for LSAs to view children's records and weekly plans, but not for parent helpers. However, parent helpers may well need to be informed of learning objectives and key vocabulary for specific lessons and activ-ities, and you may need to support class teachers in finding ways and opportunities to talk to parent helpers.

The deployment of LSAs often falls within the two pronged approach to children with individual learning needs:

- LSAs can reduce potential barriers for inclusion in learning. For example, they may be able to read instructions, act as scribes, help to modify behaviour, or present information in visual forms for children with EAL. Over-reliance on LSA support needs to be monitored, and the LSA may be used in some instances to monitor other groups of children, allowing the class teacher to work with children needing more direct support.

- LSAs can be used to administer programmes which address specific learning difficulties, such as activities that focus on the auditory memory. Where possible, these should take place within the classroom setting and should be directed by the teacher through the LSA.

These two approaches can be used to audit and analyse current LSA deployment. You may find the current provision focuses on one of the two. LSAs themselves are often the best people to evaluate their effectiveness, and their views are well worth exploring.

Meeting the needs of able or gifted and talented children

Much has been written on the identification of able, gifted and talented children, and you will find information on the world class tests at www.qca.org.uk. National tests, with their standardised scores, may be a helpful tool for identifying underperforming children. Koshy (2001) is a useful resource in this area.

Subject leaders in mathematics are often asked to support class teachers in providing activities for able children and advice as to the sort of level they should be working at. Details of a useful publication, *Mathematical Challenges for Able Pupils in Key Stages 1 and 2* (DfES, 2000) can be found at www.standards.dfes.gov.uk/numeracy/publications. This book suggests activities for children who are likely to exceed the expected standards for their year group. The activities link to key objectives taken from the NNS, allowing the whole class to work on the same area of mathematics. This book (page 4) characterises able children as those who typically:

- grasp new material quickly;
- are prepared to approach problems from different directions and persist in finding solutions;
- generalise patterns and relationships;
- use mathematical symbols confidently;
- develop concise logical arguments.

Enrichment/Acceleration

The mathematics subject leader may be pivotal in reaching a whole school decision on the management of the learning of able children. There are two options.

1. Acceleration.
Here a child is taught objectives from a year group higher than their own, either in a class with their peers or with children older than themselves.

2. Enrichment.
Here the child is kept within their own year group, and covers a broad curriculum which extends sideways from the objectives for their own NNS yearly programme.

This is often referred to as the Enrichment/Acceleration debate. Of course the needs of individual children should be evaluated on their own terms, and decisions negotiated with the children themselves, their class teachers and their parents. The following questions may help you to lead staff discussion and judge the case of each able child.

Is acceleration the best option?

- The learning of mathematics should be interactive, involving discussion and collaborative work. Is the child going to interact with members of the older group? Will there be social difficulties? What will the effect be on other children in the group? If the child is accelerated through the curriculum but kept in a teaching group with their peers, how will they interact with others? Will they have opportunities to participate in mathematical discussion, or will this be only with the teacher?
- The child who does not move onto the next school a year early will cover the Year 3 or Year 7 curriculum during their final year. How will they be able to discuss their work with peers? What opportunities will there be for interaction and use of mathematical vocabulary? Will there be a need for LSA support?
- When the child reaches the final year at the school, are there appropriate materials for Year 3 or Year 7?
- Will the child repeat the Year 3 or Year 7 curriculum in their next school? Negotiation with the next school is crucial.
- Are Year 2 and Year 6 class teachers confident in the subject knowledge needed for the next year's curriculum?
- How can parents be involved?
- How will the child react to the situation?
- Is it possible that a child may be taught alongside an older sibling? What effect will this have on both children?

Is enrichment the best option?

- Are teachers confident in their ability to provide purposeful and appropriate activities? How will they be supported?
- Does the school have access to appropriate materials?
- Will the child be isolated? Will they have opportunities to use mathematical vocabulary and interact with peers? Will there be a need for LSA support?
- Can targets be used to focus and monitor enrichment?
- How can parents be involved?
- How will the child react to the situation?

The Booster and Springboard initiatives

The Booster and Springboard initiatives represent a belief in targeted intervention to help children reach their potential and to raise the level of pupils reaching level 4 at the end of Key Stage 2.

They do of course have implications for the timetabling of teaching groups. A flexible approach to the use of these schemes can allow targeted support for groups of children. However, every child has a right to a broad and balanced curriculum, and the use of Springboard for example at the same time every week would have an impact on other subjects. Using the programmes outside the school day may be preferable, but it could be that the targeted children also receive additional support in literacy, leading to an overload. The subject leader needs to be able to look creatively at the current provision in the school, and at the Booster and Springboard schemes in order to gain the most benefit. Guidance is given through the DfES, but a firm knowledge of the school itself enables the subject leader to make, and justify, decisions about the best use of these opportunities. For example, if you are promoting a discussion on the connectionist approach to teaching, you would want to make sure that class teachers are in a position to make links between the daily mathematics lesson and the Springboard and Booster programmes. The website, www.standards.dfes.gov.uk/numeracy, provides guidance for schools in deciding how best to use these programmes.

Summary

Ensuring provision for all children's needs in mathematics presents some complex issues. Every school and every child has individual needs, and this chapter has offered some strategies to help you to address these. However, this is an area in which you will need to work closely with key members of staff such as the SENCO and other subject leaders. Your position will require you to work on two levels: first, you may be asked to address the particular needs of individual children, taking time to learn about their strengths and needs, and work with others to ensure their needs are met; second, you will need to take an overview of practices across the school, using your monitoring and staff development procedures to ensure the inclusion of, and high expectations for, all pupils.

6 THE SUBJECT LEADER'S ROLE IN LEADING THE ASSESSMENT OF MATHEMATICS

➔ The National Standards for Subject Leadership state that subject leaders should:

- analyse and interpret relevant national, local and school data, research and inspection evidence to inform policies, practices, expectations, targets and teaching methods;

- establish and implement clear policies and practices for assessing, recording and reporting on pupil achievement, and for using this information to recognise achievement and to assist pupils in setting targets for further improvement;

- ensure that information about pupils' achievements in previous classes and schools is used effectively to secure good progress in the subject.

As subject leader, you will want to play a role in using assessment to raise standards in the teaching and learning of mathematics across the school. You will need to establish your own clear understanding of the purpose of assessment and act as a reflective practitioner, offering your practice as an exemplar when necessary. At the same time, you will need to provide a leadership role in this area, working with the assessment coordinator and other subject leaders to support staff in the use of assessment to enhance teaching and learning.

You may find that your role involves:

- providing clear guidance on effective assessment and monitoring in the policy statement for mathematics;

- leading whole school INSET in such areas as sharing good practice, analysing children's errors, moderating teacher assessments;

- supporting individual teachers on an informal basis;

- analysing performance in National Tests as a means of monitoring the teaching and learning of mathematics and setting whole school targets;

- considering assessment of mathematics across the whole school perhaps by drawing up an assessment calendar which allows you to consider when and how more formal assessments take place. (See assessment calendar on page 47)

Year group	Autumn term	Spring term	Summer term
Reception	Initial assessment	Initial assessment of new intake	Foundation Stage profile
Year I			Teacher assessment
Year 2			KSI National Tests Teacher assessment
Year 3		Optional QCA tests	Teacher assessment
Year 4		Optional QCA tests	Teacher assessment
Year 5		Optional QCA tests	Teacher assessment
Year 6			Teacher assessment KS2 National Tests

An assessment calendar

Reflection

Consider the extent to which you already have developed aspects of this role.

Can you concisely describe your own view regarding the purpose of assessment?

Could you describe examples of your own use of assessment opportunities in your classroom?

Do the records you keep of the children's progress in mathematics meet the needs of the audience who need to use the information?

Do you know how assessment is undertaken in mathematics across the school?

Is there a clear policy for the whole school regarding the assessment of mathematics?

The most important purpose of assessment is to provide information to enhance the future teaching and learning of mathematics. It might be useful to think of assessment *for* learning as opposed to assessment *of* learning which is not necessarily used to inform planning. Assessment for learning may include:

- information gathered by the teacher or LSA during a lesson against the objective to help the teacher plan the next lesson;
- a child's self assessment against a lesson objective;
- gathering information through a more formal activity which assesses, for example, a week's work on fractions;

- information passed on from a previous teacher or school at the end of a year.

Assessment information is essential for those involved in the teaching and learning of mathematics – teachers, parents, children, LSAs, and occasionally other outside agencies such as educational psychologists – so sometimes it is necessary to record the information.

The NNS *Framework* (DfES, 1999) provides detailed guidance as to the assessment of mathematics in its introduction (Section 1, pages 33 to 37). However, its use of the terms short-, medium- and long-term assessments, although they link clearly to planning, are not necessarily terms which are usually associated with assessment. There may be a need to reach a shared understanding of these terms with the staff. It may be more useful to link these levels of assessment with more recognised terminology such as formative and summative assessment, or assessment for learning and assessment of learning.

- Short-term assessment can be defined as formative day-to-day assessment during or after the daily mathematics lesson. This is assessment for learning as it feeds into the following lesson.
- Medium-term assessment tends to take place at the end of a short topic or unit of work and in this sense can be defined as summative or assessment of learning. However, with the structure of the curriculum where each topic is revisited once or twice a term, medium-term assessment can also be seen as informing the next teaching of the topic. The NNS calls this 'assess and review'.
- Long-term assessment takes place at the end of the year or when each topic is taught for the last time, and can be defined as summative or assessment of learning.

This chapter considers the role of the mathematics subject leader at the three levels of assessment.

Short-term assessment

Short-term assessment is the day-to-day assessment which often happens informally and is rarely recorded. It generally takes place against the lesson's objectives. Teachers often share the lesson's objective with the children at the beginning of the lesson, explaining exactly what they will be looking for in the lesson and what they expect the children to learn. It is essential therefore to have focused, clear objectives linked to the children's previous level of understanding, and articulated to the children in a way they can understand. These can be worded in such a way as to make the success criteria clear. Objectives which use phrases such as 'know that', 'to be aware of', 'increase confidence in' are less focused than those which make use of phrases such as 'be able to identify', 'to use addition and subtraction facts to 10 to solve problems'. LSAs also need to be aware of the objective if they are to aid in collecting assessment information. An over-reliance on assessment against lesson objectives can lead to an oversimplified model of teaching, where the sequence of learning is rigidly structured by the objectives; however, an experienced teacher is able to modify lessons and assessment opportunities when learning does not fit the predicted pattern. For example, an Early Years teacher might have certain possible learning objectives in mind when they observe children at play, but will assess learning as it takes place, even if it is not as predicted.

The subject leader's role at this level is generally to be a good practitioner, able to discuss, and if necessary exhibit, good practice. You will need to consider issues surrounding good practice in this area.

Short-term assessment may take the form of:

- observation of practical work, games or play;
- assessing drawings and diagrams;
- questioning children, particularly during work with a focus group in the main activity and during the plenary of the lesson;
- marking written work.

Each of these methods will be more or less appropriate for the particular objectives and groups of children to be assessed.

Observation

Very young children can be best assessed through observation and questioning, for example when they are playing. This may be child-initiated unstructured play, where the focus of the observation may not be predetermined, or structured teacher-directed play where there is a clear focus. Observation may involve the teacher entering into the play, and conversing with the child in role. For example, the teacher may spend a short time observing a child playing in the home area during an unstructured play activity, where she is counting out plates to set the table. The teacher may note that the child does not count accurately, exhibiting a difficulty with the one to one correspondence between the number names and objects. The teacher may enter into the play, and pretend to help the child to set the table, counting the plates together. Additionally this information may be used to inform later teaching input given to all the children during sessions on the carpet. Similarly a teacher may make use of structured play to assess children's use of number bonds to ten. She may set up a small shop area where play dough biscuits cost between Ip and I0p. The children are given I0p to spend in the shop, whilst the teacher observes and assesses their discussions. She may again enter into the play activity in order to question a particular child more closely, but this is done in a playful and therefore less intimidating manner.

Experienced teachers make valuable use of informal, day-to-day assessment of this kind. Other teachers may need to be supported with the organisational issues related to the inclusion of observation such as this into their daily plan. Often an experienced teacher of the Early Years can be the best person to share their expertise, and if the mathematics subject leader is not in this position themselves, it is important that they are aware of key issues. LSAs can be an essential aid in the observation of children. Their inclusion in staff discussion on assessment through observation, and any other method, would be worth considering. It is important that LSAs have an opportunity to share and discuss information gathered with class teachers. If a recording sheet is needed, ask teachers and LSAs to draw this up together so that it meets their needs.

Assessing written work

Assessment by observation contrasts with the use of written work as assessment information. Paper and pencil evidence, whether it is in the form of writing, number sentences, drawings and diagrams, can provide assessment of a large number of children at a time. Observation, in contrast, focuses on a small number of children. However, teachers are well aware of the limitations of written work as a form of assessment. Often children's understanding is underestimated by written work, and sometimes overestimated if they are working with more able children. However, the use of written work alongside the questioning of children throughout the three part lesson, particularly during the plenary session, can be a useful compromise. It may be possible to work with a focus group during the main part of the lesson, at least for some of the time, allowing an opportunity to observe and question a group of children. OFSTED, in the report *The NNS: the First Year* (2000), identified the ineffective flitting of teachers around the classroom during this part of the lesson. They recommended that teachers' time would be better spent in direct teaching of a group. Short-term assessment of mental and oral objectives necessarily needs to be done through observation and questioning, and requires the teacher to work with a small focus group. However, this calls for certain classroom management skills. If other groups of children are to work independently, even for a small length of time in order to release the teacher to work with a focus group, the work set for them must be closely matched to their ability level. There must be clear procedures for children who finish early or 'get stuck'. For example the teacher may discuss and implement the following guidelines which can be displayed in the classroom:

> *If you are stuck, try one of these ideas.*
>
> - *Read the question again.*
> - *Underline the important words.*
> - *Try to draw a diagram or get some equipment to help you.*
> - *Ask a friend to help you.*
> - *Don't give up; remember that the best mathematicians get stuck.*
> - *Being stuck means you are just ready to learn something new.*
> - *If all else fails, find a maths puzzle to do.*
>
> *Remember, only disturb your teacher when she is working with a group if there is an emergency.*

Questioning

Discussion with both teachers and LSAs on the use of probing questions can help to share good practice. The NNS *Assess and Review* material includes some useful examples of probing questions which are linked to key objectives. Short-term assessment may not necessarily be against key objectives, but these examples may be a useful starting point to discuss the use of probing questions. For example, in a staff meeting on assessment, you might discuss one or two of the examples in the file, and then choose an objective from the school's medium-term planning in order to discuss which probing questions may be used to measure children's learning in this area. Then teachers and LSAs working in year groups could draw up a selection of questions to match particular objectives to be covered. The report *Using Assessment to Raise Achievement in Mathematics* (QCA, 2001) is available on www.qca.org.uk and provides a full discussion on the use of questions to assess learning. The NNS *Mathematical Vocabulary* book is also a useful resource. Of course, continual questioning can cause children some anxiety, and care needs to be taken to ensure that children are not over exposed to probing questions. A classroom ethos where children feel safe to answer questions, to hypothesise and to predict, is essential. The focus of the NNS on the sharing of strategies has been an important factor in establishing this ethos in many classrooms.

Whole staff discussion of probing questions may lead into INSET on the analysis of children's errors, which can offer an insight into children's understanding. The NNS offers much support in leading INSET in this area; information can be found at www.standards.dfes.gov.uk/numeracy/publications.

Reflection

Consider the information which these errors may give you about individual children's understanding:

A child in Year 1 repeatedly gives an answer which is incorrect by one such as

3 + 5 =7
2+ 4 =5

A child in Year 3 states that a rectangle split into quarters with one quarter shaded shows 1/3

A child in Year 6 says that 4.5 x 10 = 40.5.

Marking

Supporting staff in the area of short-term assessment may lead you into issues related to marking. Marking has much the same purpose as questioning. It should serve to enhance learning by measuring the strengths of written work against objectives which have been shared with the children and indicating how improvements can be made. Marking should be clear to children, parents and any other outside agencies that may be involved in the child's learning. The use of acronyms and abbreviations can cause some confusion if they are not clearly explained. Detailed marking of written work can often be ignored by children if they are not given time to reflect on it. Lesson objectives are often the focus for marking, and a lesson can be tightly structured by the objectives. The children are therefore fully aware of the teacher's expectations and how their work will be marked from the beginning of the lesson. This is particularly useful when the objectives refer to MAI where assessment can be more vague. Staff development on the specific processes of problem solving and investigative skills as detailed in MAI can help teachers to set focused objectives which can be assessed. Of course marking which solely recognises achievement in terms of the objective can miss other important learning which may be incidental, yet valuable. As the subject leader of mathematics, you will want to establish with the staff:

- good practice in terms of marking, which may mean discussing examples of your own or others' marking;

- procedures for marking work which is incorrect. The correction of too many errors can have a detrimental effect on self-esteem, although parents or inspectors should be able to see how these errors are tackled by the teacher and child. The teacher may indicate in the child's book that individual help will be given;

- appropriate use of positive comments which are understood by the child, to build self confidence;

- clear procedures for marking work relating to MAI;

- strategies to deal with the volume of marking such as the appropriate use of marking during the plenary.

The QCA website is a good resource in terms of current research in this area.

Medium-term assessment

The purpose of medium-term assessment is to provide summative information at the end of a topic or unit of work, where children's learning is measured against wider objectives. This information is usually recorded as it acts as formative assessment for the next time the particular unit is taught, which could be later in the term or year. Often this sort of assessment acts as a reinforcement of short-term assessment, providing more formal evidence of intuitive informal judgements. Medium-term assessment can also provide more detailed evidence for the children who appear to be more difficult to assess on an everyday basis, perhaps because their learning is more erratic, or they are quiet by nature and rarely offer answers during whole class or group discussions. In practice, close assessment may only be necessary for a small number of children.

The NNS states clearly that it is not necessary to assess and record each child's progress against every objective. Medium-term assessments are usually against key objectives which are much more general yet serve to provide useful information for future teaching.

As in the case of short-term assessment, it is often the role of the subject leader to be a good practitioner in this area, confident to try and evaluate critically new ideas and strategies, and to share good practice across the school. Medium-term assessments can take the form of:

- written activities which are designed to show progress against the relevant key objective. The children are asked to work individually on this occasion, to show what they have learnt. The activities are seen as part of the children's everyday experience as much as possible. Some schools ask the subject leader to supply these activities. Where this is the case, it is important that teachers have the flexibility to adapt activities to meet the needs of the children. For example, there may be individual children who will not perform well in purely written tasks due to specific learning needs;

- paper and pencil tests which again are designed to measure progress against key objectives. These activities are more formal in nature and may cause increased anxiety in the children. They may provide more accurate information in that there will be no opportunity at all for children to collaborate, but this must be weighed against the effect of possible anxiety;

- written assessments are not effective with young children, or children with specific learning difficulties. In these cases, practical activities can be designed, and the children asked to perform these, possibly in small groups, whilst the teacher observes, questions and records evidence of progress. This process is time consuming but gives a more thorough insight into learning.

Examples of recording sheets against the key objectives are available on the Standards website, and can be modified to meet the needs of individual schools, classes or children.

The NNS makes provision in sample medium-term plans for Assess and Review lessons at the end of each half term, for medium-term assessment. As subject leader, you may wish to discuss the use of these with your staff. Teachers of the Early Years in particular may wish to undertake medium-term assessments more regularly than this, at the end of each week or two weeks, immediately after the learning has been reinforced. In this case, the Assess and Review lessons are spread evenly throughout the year. Other teachers may wish to assess at the end of each half term to measure the ability of children to sustain learning. Guidance is given in *Using Assess and Review Lessons* (DfES, 2001).

The nature of medium-term assessment sometimes causes frustration in teachers. If assessment takes place during the last day of a unit of work, or the last day of term, and the teacher uncovers misconceptions, there is little or no time to address them. Usually there are few surprises: teachers find that the medium-term assessment confirms what they already know. When misconceptions are discovered, the LSA may need to work with individuals, or the mental and oral starter could be used to revise and reinforce concepts with the whole class.

Information gathered through medium- and short-term assessment can be used for target setting. Targets may be appropriate for groups of children or for individuals who do not easily fit into ability groups. Accurate assessment will ensure that these targets are specific, realistic and achievable.

Self-assessment can be used as a source of extra information for the teacher, and perhaps more importantly as a means of offering children an opportunity to increase their responsibility for their own learning and to reflect on learning itself. Self-assessment can happen quite informally during the plenary of the daily mathematics lesson. Written self-assessment can take place at the short-term assessment level, but when little time is left for real reflection and discussion with the teacher, it tends to be perfunctory. Continual use of worksheets which always ask children to indicate the level of their understanding are an example of this. Therefore self-assessment lends itself best to medium-term assessment, at the end of a topic or unit of work, which is a natural time to reflect and evaluate. This might coincide with the completion of children's targets.

Other strategies can be used where particular topics have not been revisited for a longer period of time, and the teacher wants to check that learning has been sustained. For example, concept mapping, where the children could be asked to record everything they know about fractions, can assist the teacher in planning a week's work in this area.

As subject leader, you may occasionally need to lead informal or formal INSET in the area of medium-term assessment. The NNS provides guidance here in the form of Professional Development Materials (which can be found on the Standards website) and in the Assess and Review folder. This folder contains sample lesson plans for assessment lessons against key objectives and video footage which might promote useful discussion with the staff about the nature of medium-term assessment. You might ask some teachers to try these lessons and provide some feedback. Issues relating to probing questions may also be discussed. The aim of such a session will be to establish a shared understanding of the nature of effective medium-term assessments, how these may be recorded, and to share good practice. The policy statement can then include resulting agreements.

Reflection

Can you be sure that the evidence you feel shows that a child has met a particular key objective would be accepted by other teachers within your school?

An important part of your role as subject leader will be to ensure moderation of medium-term assessments. *Standards in Mathematics* (QCA, 1999) provides examples of activities and children's work linked to each key objective. A staff meeting may allow you to discuss some of these examples, in order to unpick exactly your shared understanding of the key objectives, and what would provide evidence that children have achieved them. It is very important that evidence is not purely written work, and that all children have access to assessment activities. The examples in this publication are not exhaustive but they are useful in providing a starting point for discussion. Teachers may, within year groups, design activities to match the key objectives to be covered which meet the needs of their particular classes. These could be trialled and a later meeting could provide feedback. Examples of children's work which the staff agree do show evidence that a key objective has been met could be kept centrally in the staff room, acting as a bank of ideas and moderation for the future. In this way, the *Standards in Mathematics* booklet will be extended and tailored for your school.

Long-term assessment

Long-term assessment takes place at the end of the academic year and is summative in the sense that it records progress over the whole year, but should also be formative as it should be used in the planning of the child's next steps. Long-term assessment occurs at a time when teachers are most tired, but have access to a wealth of information on each child.

Reflection

Which sorts of long-term assessment information have been most useful to you when planning for a new class in September?

What should long-term assessment consist of?

- Long-term assessment should include the collection and completion of medium-term assessment against all the key objectives. These are then used by the next teacher, although most teachers recognise the effects on learning of a holiday away from school. Record sheets against key objectives can be downloaded from the Standards web page.

- At the end of Key Stages 1 and 2, there should also be a teacher assessment against the National Curriculum level descriptors, and statutory testing using National Tests. Some schools use the non-statutory QCA tests for Years 3, 4 and 5, and ask teachers to make teacher assessments at the end of each year. At the end of Reception Year, teachers are expected to compile the Foundation Stage Profile. Data from these, and National Tests, can be used to monitor the school's progress, and to set whole school or professional development targets.

- As a result of long-term assessment, progress is reported to parents. (For a fuller discussion on parental involvement in children's learning, see Chapter 8.)

The key objective/level descriptors debate

From the description above, it can be seen that long-term assessment seems to measure progress against both key objectives and the National Curriculum level descriptors. The key objectives for each year can be mapped onto the level descriptors:

Key Objectives	National Curriculum levels
Year 1	level 1 and start on level 2
Year 2	consolidation of level 2 and start on level 3
Year 3	revision of level 2, but mainly level 3
Year 4	consolidation of level 3 and start on level 4
Year 5	revision of level 3, but mainly level 4
Year 6	consolidation of level 4 and start on level 5

Taken from *Using key objectives, National Curriculum level descriptions and National Curriculum optional tests at Key Stages 1, 2 and 3 in Mathematics* (DfES, 2001).

The table above gives a convincing argument that the two aspects of assessment are closely linked and should give corresponding results. So why assess against both? The status of league tables and target setting has given a higher profile to the use of level descriptors, which has resulted in the use of teacher assessments in some schools at the end of each year, although this is not a statutory requirement. There has been some research which suggests that there are flaws in the use of levels of attainment as measures of achievement (Wiliam, 2001). The NNS emphasises the importance of assessment against key objectives as this gives much more detailed information about each child's learning, and is therefore much easier to use as formative assessment. The fact that a child's progress is best described as a certain National Curriculum level is less useful in that it does not state exactly what the child has achieved and where there are areas still to be developed.

You might find it helpful to read the DfES leaflet *Using key objectives, National Curriculum level descriptions and National Curriculum optional tests at Key Stages 1, 2 and 3 in Mathematics*.

The subject leader's role in moderating teacher assessments

Teacher assessments are against each Attainment Target and involve best-fit judgements. DfES guidelines show how the teacher assessments are used to provide an overall level, as the weighting of some Attainment Targets can differ. Teacher assessments can be confirmed by National Tests results, but may not necessarily be identical. The National Tests provide a snapshot picture of the achievements of children, generally on a pencil and paper test. Teacher assessments are the result of many interactions and observations, and provide a much fuller picture of the child's achievements over the breadth of the mathematics curriculum. The National Tests do not, of course, provide opportunities for detailed assessment of MA1. Some teachers may be anxious when there is a difference between the National Tests result and the teacher assessment, and may need convincing on this point. The school should be able to justify such a difference through medium-term assessment records, evidence of children's work and the teacher's knowledge of the child.

The subject leader will have a role in supporting individual teachers in the process of reaching a teacher assessment, and in providing a form of moderation. For example, it may be possible to consider a full range of one child's work and information from the class teacher during a staff meeting, and reach a joint teacher assessment. Such a discussion will allow you to reach a common understanding of the breadth of the information which can be used, and establish examples of evidence for level descriptors.

National tests

These provide long-term assessment which is standardised and reliable to a certain extent as there is little or no scope for children to collaborate. They provide generally objective information, alongside the more subjective teacher assessment, to complete the summative assessment picture. They show exactly how a child can perform on a given day in a relatively formal test setting. In Key Stage 2 in particular, they do not show how the child approaches mathematics in a variety of contexts, how they can discuss, collaborate, reflect or use the full range of skills of MAI. Their value therefore is limited, although their status is often high. It is important therefore, although it may be difficult, for you as the subject leader to maintain the balance between teacher assessments and statutory testing.

Some research has questioned the validity of the National Tests, suggesting that some of the questions asked are not equally accessible for children of differing backgrounds, and for boys and girls. Further information on this can be found in Cooper and Dunne (2000).

Reflection

Have the National Tests provided information which you have been able to use in your future planning?

The use of QCA optional tests in Years 3, 4 and 5 can provide summative information which may be used to track individual children or make predictions for end of Key Stage whole school targets. The standardised scores which can be calculated from these tests are useful in order to identify children who underachieve in the classroom or who may need extra support. You may also use these tests as formative assessment. For example, if these tests are administered during rather than at the end of the year, the information they provide can be used by class teachers to guide medium-term planning. Furthermore, you, in the role of subject leader, may use the tests as a source of monitoring information. For example, a quick survey of the children's papers may enable you to:

• monitor progress in specific areas such as number or data handling across Key Stage 2. This may supply more concrete evidence for intuitive feelings you already have after your initial audit of mathematics and feed into your subject development plan, or act as a success criterion for a target on which you have been working;

• measure the success of girls against boys within your school to consider teaching and learning styles;

• compare the achievements of your school with those of similar schools using data available on the QCA website;

• measure the success of children who, for example, may be in the same year group but be taught in different contexts. For example, you may have introduced setting and want to monitor closely its success. I have in the past used this information to monitor year groups which have been split and taught with other age ranges. In the case of a small school, Year 4 children were split into Year 3/4 and Year 4/5 classes. The staff were anxious to monitor the progress of the two groups of Year 4 children in the two classes, and the QCA tests alongside teacher assessments allowed us to do this.

The reports on *The Standards at Key Stage I in English and Mathematics* and on *The*

Standards at Key Stage 2 on English, Mathematics and Science (QCA, 2001) provide an analysis of all children's performance on each of the questions in the National Tests and can be used to compare your own children's achievements with the national picture of attainment.

The high status of National Tests and the publication of schools' results have inevitably led to a rise in the time spent in preparation for testing. You may be asked to support teachers in this, and will need to take advice from your head teacher as to the extent to which children should be trained to answer questions likely to occur in the tests. Particularly in Key Stage 2, the National Test papers do provide a bank of problem solving activities which can be useful. QCA provide advice as to how to prepare children appropriately for the National Tests.

Whole School Target Setting

You may be involved along with the senior management of the school in setting targets for the school's future performance in mathematics at the end of each Key Stage. Full and detailed guidance for this is provided by QCA. Through an analysis of the available data, value added information can be monitored for individual children, classes and year groups. There are formulas for making predictions of future achievements. Although National Tests provide useful information for target setting and the prediction of future performance, this does need to be balanced with teachers' knowledge of the individual children.

Comparing your own results with those of similar schools, and the national average, can provide some information to add to your initial and ongoing subject audit. The use of such data will not be your only form of monitoring as it is quite limited, but it may confirm your own findings. You could for example compare your own data with national figures, found on the Standards website, in order to monitor the performance of the boys and girls in your school. You could compare results from the QCA tests in Years 3, 4 and 5 to give a more detailed picture of performance. Therefore whole school results are valuable in adding to the subject leader's audit of the teaching and learning of mathematics across the school, confirming but not necessarily replacing the intuitive feeling the subject leader can gain from working alongside teachers and talking with them formally and informally.

Transferring information to new teachers and schools

The results of long-term assessment often need to be sent to new schools or teachers for the beginning of the academic year. When the change is within the school, this can be straightforward. Written long-term assessment information can be balanced with teachers' more informal comments on social development, the ability to work with others in mathematics lessons, approach to practical, open-ended activities etc. This information may be essential in planning the children's first experiences in the new class. You may have a role in co-ordinating with the head of mathematics in the local secondary school, or the mathematics subject leader of the infant, junior or middle school, to ensure that when the children change school the most useful information is passed to the teachers who will need to use it. Inviting the teachers of mathematics from new schools to work with children before the summer holidays can help to ease the transition. Joint use of the QCA *Bridging Units in Mathematics* and the Transition Units can also help provide a sense of continuity in the learning of mathematics between Key Stages 2 and 3.

Summary

Assessment is central to effective teaching and learning of mathematics. However, the processes of assessment and record keeping can be time-consuming and quite baffling for newly qualified and less experienced teachers. Support from the subject leader is important. You will be able to share efficient but effective practices through critical evaluation of your own beliefs and assessment strategies, and by establishing a climate where colleagues discuss assessment issues and learn from each other.

7 CO-ORDINATING THE USE OF INFORMATION AND COMMUNICATION TECHNOLOGY WITHIN MATHEMATICS

➔ The National Standards for Subject Leadership state that subject leaders should:

- ensure the effective and efficient management and organisation of learning resources, including information and communication technology;
- organise and co-ordinate the deployment of learning resources, including information and communication technology, and monitor their effectiveness.

Information and communication technology (ICT) represents a range of resources that can be extremely useful in the teaching and learning of mathematics. I have devoted this chapter to these resources, as they are unique in the contributions they can make, and in the range of attitudes teachers have towards them.

Just as any other resource, two important questions should be applied to the use of ICT:

- Is ICT the best resource to aid the children to meet the learning objective of the lesson?
- If not, which other resources would be more appropriate?

There is often some pressure from head teachers and ICT subject leaders to ensure that computers in classrooms are always in use, and that ICT suites are fully utilised, as these represent such large proportions of the total money spent on teaching resources. ICT, of course, is not always the best resource for a particular lesson's objectives. However, the mathematics subject leader is responsible for ensuring that class teachers are fully aware of the learning objectives which can best be supported by ICT, in order that they may make informed decisions about its use.

Reflection

Consider your own view of the advantages of ICT as a resource.

ICT, where it is defined as the use of the computer, can be thought of as offering the following opportunities:

1. presenting an extra source of motivation. This is particularly important when continuous consolidation is necessary and a new context for learning is required (for example, the program Toy Shop);

2. providing a context which immediately corrects children's errors, acting rather like a teacher or LSA when these can not be present. However, the computer

cannot be fully interactive in its response to children, and can usually only offer a right or wrong response (for example, the program Carroll Diagram);

3. allowing animation which may enhance learning but which would not be possible otherwise (for example, the program What's my Angle?);

4. providing in some cases graphing packages which release children from the manual task of drawing graphs, allowing them to tackle the important skill of graph interpretation, whilst modelling the accurate drawing of graphs (for example the program Handy Graph);

5. offering unique open ended contexts for learning such as RM Nimbus Super Logo and spreadsheet packages;

6. opening up a range of activities, tasks, competitions and information through the internet.

(All examples for I to 4 are taken from the DfES CD ROM *Using ICT to Support Mathematics in Primary Schools*)

The definition of ICT purely as the use of the computer is very limited. ICT can also be seen to include:

- calculators;
- listening centres;
- digital cameras;
- video;
- TV broadcasts;
- overhead projectors and transparencies;
- Roamers or Pips;

and many more.

Good practice

As with all areas of mathematics, the subject leader will need to act as an example of a reflective practitioner. The subject leader's open yet critical approach is not only necessary, but should also be evident to all members of staff. It is useful therefore to consider some examples of good practice in the use of ICT to enhance teaching and learning.

- The objective for a Reception class is to use language to describe the shape and size of flat shapes and to begin to name a circle, triangle, square and rectangle. During the mental and oral work the children sing number and shape rhymes. The teacher then reminds the children about their previous work on flat shapes and together they talk about shapes around their room, and name them. During the day the children complete activities which involve shape. Some of them work with play dough and cutters of different shapes. They are invited to make some biscuits for a teddy bear tea party. They work independently but from time to time the teacher observes, assesses and talks to them about the biscuits. Another group goes around the school with a LSA who uses a digital camera to take pictures of shapes they notice on their walk. During the plenary towards the end of the day the children look at the large printed-out photographs and identify the shapes. These are made into a display which is used in following lessons.

- The objective of a Year 2 lesson is for the children to use mathematical vocabulary to describe position, direction and movement, and to recognise whole, half and quarter turns, to the left or right, clockwise or anti-clockwise. The teacher begins with a mental and oral starter where the children stand up, and consolidate left and right, whole, half and quarter turns by moving according to instructions. Then the teacher gives a teaching input on clockwise and anti-clockwise. She asks one child to be a blindfolded volunteer, and the children give this child instructions to move around the room, using the key vocabulary. This is repeated with the Roamer. The children then are set activities in mixed ability groups, as discussion and vocabulary are a feature of the lesson. One group works with the Roamer, directing it through a maze drawn out with masking tape on the floor. Another group writes instructions in pairs for moving around the classroom. A third group creates mazes for a small toy on squared paper, and then writes instructions for the toy. The plenary tries out some of the second group's instructions for moving around the room, consolidating the use of vocabulary, and clockwise and anti-clockwise in particular. Following lessons allow other groups of children to have direct experience of the Roamer.

- A Year 3 teacher has been working for some time to ensure that the children are able to partition a three digit number and know the value of each digit. The class have worked with place value cards, the software Developing Numbers (available from the Association of Teachers of Mathematics) and hundreds, tens and units equipment. One group are still finding this difficult, while the majority of the class have developed a fascination for much larger numbers. The teacher plans to use the calculators as a teaching aid. During the main part of the lesson, she models a game called Space Invaders using an overhead projector calculator. She asks one child to type in a three digit number, and then she asks the rest of the class how they might 'zap' each of the digits using a subtraction. The following discussions consolidate the learning objectives. The children play the game in pairs, with the size of the numbers acting as differentiation. During the plenary two of the children show how they worked with larger numbers, with the teacher emphasising the units, tens and hundreds parts of these numbers. The calculator game has provided a motivating activity to consolidate on going learning objectives.

- The objective of a Year 6 lesson is to calculate angles around a point. The children have been using RM Nimbus Super Logo and are familiar with the repeat command and with writing simple procedures. During the mental and oral work, the teacher asks the children in pairs to write simple procedures for drawing squares and rectangles using repeats. This acts as revision of earlier lessons. The children then sit where they can see the computer monitor. Space may be limited but they will sit in this way for a short time, whilst the teacher gives the teaching input. She types in one of the children's procedures for a square. She sets the class the challenge of drawing the square in a repeating pattern so that it overlaps and rotates round a point. They do this manually at first. Then the children are asked if they could write another procedure, using a repeat to create the pattern. The children work in pairs and write their ideas on paper. As an extension, they design procedures to create similar patterns with triangles and hexagons. During the plenary, they gather round the monitor again to try a selection of their ideas. (In an ICT suite, each pair would try their ideas straight on to the computers.)

Reflection

What in your view is an example of poor use of ICT?

Inappropriate use of ICT in teaching mathematics

It may be useful to contrast the examples discussed above with a more limited use of ICT. For example, the role of ICT in learning can be restricted when it is not closely matched to a particular objective. This is sometimes seen when the only use of ICT is the choice of closed, computer games as an activity for early finishers or as part of 'golden time'. If ICT activities are not evaluated and matched to the learning needs of the children, then the outcomes tend to be ad hoc. The child may be occupied, and may enjoy the experience, but the element of mathematical learning is left in some cases to chance.

Other examples of poor use of ICT could be seen as missed opportunities, where ICT may not be chosen but is an appropriate resource.

Poor use of ICT can be caused by:

- teachers' lack of technical knowledge of ICT leading to a lack of confidence;
- teachers' lack of experience of using ICT in the classroom, resulting in an inability to evaluate the potential and limitations of ICT;
- a mismatch between the demands of the ICT resource and the children's mathematical or ICT capability;
- continual pressure on teachers to use ICT.

These areas can be remedied through staff development, whether formally in staff meetings or informally through one to one support sessions. The NNS offers support through the Professional Development materials. The mathematics and ICT subject leaders will need to work closely together. The subject development plan for ICT may well link to that of mathematics. ICT is an area where confidence and subject knowledge are closely linked. Therefore, informal support may be most effective where it links with other programmes such as New Opportunities Funding (NOF) training.

In cases where staff are unsure how to link mathematics with ICT, it may be useful to look closely at medium-term plans with individual teachers towards the beginning of a term, and to annotate them with possible links to ICT. For example, software available in school will lend itself to particular objectives, and if you have a good knowledge of these links, you will be able to make helpful suggestions – links can be made to the use of the Roamer to objectives in the areas of shape, space and measures. Where staff are unsure of these resources, the mathematics or ICT subject leader can provide support. The use of ICT can be monitored through weekly planning, and evaluated by teachers at a staff meeting at the end of term or year.

In your role as mathematics subject leader, you may find yourself supporting staff with organising the use of computers. There are several possible models:

An ICT suite

A large ICT suite lends itself to the incorporation of ICT into whole class numeracy lessons. Mental and oral work may take place in the suite or in the classroom before entering the suite if this maximises use of the computer facilities. A projector and screen, if available, or a well positioned monitor allow the teacher to model the use of software in the teaching input. The children can then work in small groups using the software, perhaps at different levels allowing for differentiation. The plenary again can make use of the screen or one monitor to allow the class to work together. It may be necessary to make use of parent helpers as an extra support with classes of younger children who may find the ICT demands of the work difficult.

An ICT suite which does not cater for the whole class is less useful. Here the mental and oral work and teaching input may take place within the classroom, and the class split into two groups. One group could work in the ICT suite with the LSA or class teacher, and receive a teaching input there as a group. The plenary would draw the class back together.

An ICT suite is a whole school resource, and there may be tensions with its time-tabling. The staff will need to decide as a whole if it would be effective to have a complete week every term when they have the use of the suite during the numeracy lesson, or whether one day in each week or fortnight would be more useful. Early organisation of the ICT suite timetable allows the integration of ICT into medium-term planning.

One or more computers in the classroom

Computers in the classroom lend themselves to close and continual integration of ICT into the teaching and learning of mathematics, but create some organisational difficulties. Here the computers can still be used to support whole class teaching input with a data projector and screen, or by sitting the class where they can see the monitor, if only for a very short time. In this way, the computer software can be modelled by the teacher or used to support teaching. During the children's activities, one group of children could work on the computer, whilst the others work on related tasks. For example, in a Key Stage 2 class learning about counting in steps of 0.1, one group could use the program Counter (available on the DfES CD ROM as above), whilst others use calculators. Large numbers of children can find it difficult to use the computer at one time. Where there is only one computer in the classroom, it may be easier for half a group to use it for a shorter time. Where space allows, a computer can be borrowed for a week from another class, allowing a larger number of children to work with ICT during the numeracy lesson. During the following week, both computers can then be passed to the other class, allowing again a block of time with ICT and mathematics for the second class.

An ICT suite and computers in the classroom or a set of laptops to be used in any classroom

This is of course the best option, allowing for effective and flexible links between ICT and mathematics, making use of all of the strategies described so far.

You may find Fox et al (2000) useful when considering the issues relating to using ICT in mathematics lessons.

Health and safety

As the subject leader for mathematics, you should consider your share of responsibility for health and safety issues concerning ICT. Care should be taken when using the internet with children, and in evaluating the space around the computer, chair height, lighting and the length of time any child spends on the computer.

Calculators

As part of your role as subject leader of mathematics you will certainly want to establish a shared understanding of the effective use of calculators. This will be an important part of the school's policy towards the teaching of calculations and will be an essential part of the policy statement for mathematics. This is also an issue which may need to be discussed with parents.

In our discussion of calculations, the emphasis so far has been on using flexible and effective strategies which are best suited to the problem to be solved. Clearly, a calculator strategy is sometimes most appropriate. You and your staff need to agree when it is appropriate to use a calculator. The NNS policy on this is clearly stated in the Professional Development Materials relating to ICT as:

The calculator as a teaching aid

- *The calculator can help children to understand key concepts such as place value or the relationship between fractions and decimals*
- *For this purpose, it may be used at appropriate times in any year group*

The calculator as a calculating aid

- *The calculator should not be used for calculations that children can do efficiently and accurately either mentally or with pencil and paper*
- *The calculator's use as a calculating aid will mostly occur from Year 5 onward*

(Professional Development Material: Developing Mathematics in Years 4, 5 and 6, page 96)

Staff will need to reach a common understanding of this policy, and may need support in distinguishing between activities which use the calculator as a teaching aid and as a calculating aid. It may be useful to build up a bank of each type of activity, matching the activities to possible learning objectives. A possible format for a staff meeting would be to ask teachers to bring their favourite calculator activities, and to establish how they can be used as a teaching or calculating aid (this definition is often open to interpretation). Each activity can then be clearly linked to objectives located in the NNS or the school's medium-term planning, allowing for a sense of progression.

The following examples may be useful for you to establish for yourself a clear definition of the use of a calculator as a teaching aid and a calculating aid.

Using the calculator as a teaching aid:

A teacher might ask the children to multiply some single digit numbers by ten on a calculator to consolidate their understanding of the way in which the digits move to the left when numbers become ten times bigger.

Children may use the constant button on the calculator to investigate patterns in the 4 times table.

In these activities, there is a clear learning objective, and the calculator is used as a resource to help the children to reach these objectives.

Using the calculator as a calculating aid:

A teacher might ask the children to roll a die 30 times each and record the frequency of each score. They then present their findings using some of the data handling techniques they have learned previously. In order to tackle the misconception that some numbers are harder to score than others, the teacher asks all the children in the class to add their results together, presenting a large class bar chart of results which show a more even distribution of scores. Some children use a calculator to total their results as these involve larger numbers than they are able to add mentally or on paper.

A class might use a calculator to change fractions to decimal numbers in order to check an activity where they order a set of fractions and place them on a number line.

These activities have objectives which may require quite complex calculations, but the calculations themselves are not part of the objective. Therefore the calculator is a useful resource.

Sometimes, lesson objectives need to refer directly to the calculator. Children must be taught the actual skills necessary to use the calculator correctly, and these should be evident in the medium-term planning for Years 5 and 6. These skills will include:

- checking calculations by using inverse operations;
- rounding answers and interpreting solutions;
- use of the memory for problems with more than one operation.

It is essential that children are familiar with these skills before they face Paper B of the National Tests in Year 6.

To be able to assess and evaluate calculation strategies, including the use of a calculator, and to choose the most appropriate is an important skill for children to acquire. Therefore you will need to establish a shared understanding of when the calculator is an appropriate strategy. A useful activity to help the children make decisions about when to use a calculator is 'Beat the Calculator'. Two children attempt a calculation, one mentally and one on the calculator to see which one is quicker. The class then build up a bank of calculations which they know are best performed mentally.

When purchasing calculators for the school, you will need to make important decisions about which ones to buy. Calculators are not expensive, but need to be replaced quite regularly, so it is worth considering exactly how they will be used. Which functions are necessary for each Key Stage? The memory function will be important for Year 6 but will be an unnecessary confusion for younger children. Is it best to buy class sets with a matching overhead projector calculator to enable whole class teaching? Would it be useful to have at least one example of a calculator with algebraic systems in the school? This type of calculator can deal with more than one operation at a time, carries out multi-step calculations in the correct order and rounds answers. The basic calculator, which is of more use in the primary classroom, has arithmetical operating systems, and deals with one operation at a time, truncating answers. It also often has a constant memory which is useful for generating patterns.

Calculators are a useful resource to support children with individual learning needs. Children can be released from certain calculations which they find difficult, to work with real life data and very large numbers and those with several digits after the decimal point. More able children can consider how calculations which are generally beyond the capabilities of a basic calculator can be solved, and explore the priority of brackets and the four operations with an algebraic calculator.

The NNS provides very useful materials to support your own understanding and staff development in the area of calculators which can be found on www.standards.dfes. gov. uk/numeracy/publications.

Television broadcasts

An ICT resource that is often used in the primary classroom is the television broadcast. There are some very good programmes available, and these should not be overlooked.

The advantages of television broadcasts are the motivation and enthusiasm which they trigger in children, and the level of animation they provide. Good programmes make use of moving pictures and real life contexts outside the classroom, which a teacher cannot easily provide. In this sense they can be a very effective part of the teaching input of the numeracy lesson. However, they can never be truly interactive. They can ask questions of children, but cannot enter into discussion or meet individual needs. This is the teacher's skill.

Therefore, short parts of television programmes can be used very effectively in the teaching part of the lesson, when they are complemented with discussion led by the teacher. They will also need to be modified to match the exact objectives of the lesson and learning needs of the children. Showing complete programmes can be less effective, and may be better used outside the numeracy lesson as a reinforcement of learning.

Summary

Perhaps more than in any other area, the success of ICT lies in the attitudes and levels of confidence of your staff. The pairing up of mathematics and ICT may present difficulties for staff due to a lack of confidence in either or both subjects. Any change which involves teachers' beliefs and levels of confidence takes time and patience, and you should not hope to implement instant developments. You will need to convince some staff that ICT really can enhance the teaching and learning of mathematics.

8 INVOLVING PARENTS IN THEIR CHILDREN'S LEARNING

The National Standards for Subject Leadership state that subject leaders should:

- establish a partnership with parents to involve them in their child's learning of the subject, as well as providing information about curriculum, attainment, progress and targets;

- communicate effectively, orally and in writing, with parents, governors, external agencies and the wider community, including business and industry.

In my experience, a large majority of parents actively wish to support their children's learning of mathematics, but often require help to do so. They may voice concern about 'doing it the wrong way' or not understanding 'the way maths is done these days'. With support from the subject leader, the powerful force which parents represent can be harnessed to enhance the learning of mathematics.

'Parents are a child's first and enduring teachers. They play a crucial role in helping their children learn. Children achieve more when schools and parents work together. Parents can help more effectively if they know what the school is trying to achieve and how they can help.' www.standards.dfes.gov.uk

This chapter will consider exactly how a subject leader can practically involve and engage parents in children's learning of mathematics.

Informing parents

By informing parents and guardians, you enable them to work alongside the school and support children's learning. Parents need to be aware of your general beliefs in the nature of mathematics and the sorts of learning you hope to promote. For example, some parents may have experienced through their own education a procedural approach to written calculations. They may have been taught certain written methods for addition, subtraction, multiplication and division, but never explored the way in which the methods work or really understood the mathematics underpinning them. They may use an equal addition method for subtraction rather than the now more common methods of decomposition or complementary addition. Therefore, you may need to describe the way in which your school promotes understanding of number and emphasises mental calculations and written methods which are refined to become increasingly effective and efficient.

As well as imparting your general beliefs, parents need to be informed of specific issues relating to mathematics such as:

- a change in the published scheme used by the school;
- the use of calculators;
- the importance of homework and the way in which homework enriches learning in school;
- implementation of new government initiatives;
- setting targets for children's learning.

Often parents can be informed of straightforward issues through newsletters written in a friendly style, excluding technical language which may not be understood by the majority of parents. It is a good idea to discuss the style and tone of your letters with a parent or colleague. You can easily miss a mistake or make an assumption that another reader will be able to pinpoint for you. Of course final drafts should involve your head teacher and perhaps the governor with responsibility for mathematics.

Newsletters provide information but do not lend themselves to an interactive discussion with parents. Nor do they allow you to really challenge beliefs and promote your own ideas effectively. Information evenings or workshops can be a time consuming but more dynamic alternative. Many adults have negative feelings towards mathematics; consequently there is a need not only to inform parents but also to promote a positive attitude to the subject. It may take time and care to provide reassurance and encouragement, and this can involve a parents' meeting or workshop.

Parents' meetings are ideal forums for you not only to disseminate important information, but also to discuss issues. Given encouragement, parents will express their own views, and in some cases concerns, enabling you to share your beliefs and ideas. For example, after a parental consultation evening you might feel that some parents are anxious about the way calculators are used in mathematics lessons. Other members of staff might reinforce your views with examples of comments from parents of children in their classes. This may have been an area of previous staff development, identified in your audit and subject development plan. Therefore a workshop for parents might be arranged.

A workshop implies that parents themselves are going to engage in some work. Of course some parents will be worried by this, anticipating failure and public humiliation. You will need to advertise the evening in such a way as to assure parents that this will not happen. The activities you ask the parents to work on should be non-threatening, but purposeful. You will need to link the activities to the children's learning so that their value is clear. Inviting children to work alongside their parents shows how the three parties – teacher, child and parent – are working together to the same end. Children may also encourage their parents to attend. You could set up different activities on tables in a classroom or the hall, which the parents and children try together. Working in small groups can help to support those parents who are less confident in their own mathematical ability. Each activity would need to be supervised by a class teacher. A final plenary would allow you to show how the activities are used to enhance children's learning in the classroom, and state the school's policy towards the use of calculators.

Another important issue that parents need to know about is the school's calculation strategy. Again, gathering evidence of parental interest and possible concerns can help you to persuade the head teacher and staff that a parents' evening or workshop would be valuable. This is the area in which you will require much support from parents with homework, and in which parents' own experience of mathematics may be significantly different to that of their children. Again, a workshop rather than a newsletter allows a forum for discussion. Parents will come with a variety of calculation strategies themselves, a fact which will enable you to show the importance of flexible and efficient mental strategies. You will also need to show how standard written methods are taught in a way which links to mental methods whenever possible to ensure that they are based on understanding. The NNS Professional Development Materials include OHTs and ideas which may well be useful. The workshop should allow opportunities for parents to make calculations and to reflect on their own strategies. You will be able to discuss how children need to be armed with a range of strategies which can be matched to solving individual problems. You might also show the sorts of mistakes that children make with standard written methods when these are not fully understood. For example:

$$
\begin{array}{r}
2\ \ 5\ \ 6 \\
+\ \ 7\ \ 8 \\
\hline
9\ \ 13\ \ 6
\end{array}
$$

You will want to stress, however, that it is important to introduce children to formal written methods as these are powerful, compact methods which are very useful with large numbers and those with several digits after the decimal point. By the end of the evening, you will want to explain the whole school strategy towards calculation, and perhaps give some ideas of activities which can be used at home to support children's understanding.

The issues for discussion with parents can often be controversial. For example, there may be parents with very strong views about the use of calculators who try to dominate the meeting. This should not deter you from holding the event, but requires you to be well prepared. Consider beforehand the sorts of comments or questions which are likely to be most difficult such as:

Children can come to rely on calculators.

Why don't you teach tables like we were taught them?

Any of these issues can be answered if you are prepared and you have discussed them in your formulation of the mathematics policy or whole school scheme of work. Of course it is important that all the staff have the same beliefs, so that you promote a shared vision. Your head teacher in particular should be there to support you with any difficult questions which relate to wider issues. Talking to a selection of parents informally before the meeting can give you an insight into the sort of concerns parents have. If you are concerned about difficult questions, you may feel more comfortable if you invite an LEA advisor, NNS consultant or outside speaker to support you. However, it is important that you agree with visiting speakers beforehand on the policies you aim to promote and that you are prepared to answer questions that relate to your school in particular.

Parent meetings inevitably do not include all the parents, and you may wish to send a newsletter home to all parents after the event, summarising the discussion.

Homework

Homework, or out of class work as it is sometimes known, can of course provide an ongoing means of involving parents in their children's learning of mathematics. Homework can also give rise to considerable anxiety for both children and their parents.

Reflection

Consider an example of homework which has been very successful. How has it contributed to learning within the classroom? Did the task have to be completed at home, or was it an extra task, which just happened to take place at home?

As a mathematics subject leader, you will need to establish, firstly for yourself, principles of effective homework in your subject. The school may have a homework policy based on government guidelines, but you will want to have an input into the types of mathematical tasks which are used for homework. The following points may help to clarify your thoughts:

- What opportunities to learn mathematics lie in the home, garden, or any part of the child's environment out of school? Generally, homework can provide a 'real life' dimension to learning – for example, exploring prices in real shops, distances between real places, capacities of real food packages etc. Can homework capitalise on these opportunities? Some homework tasks simply replicate the child's work in the classroom, such as completing a worksheet on number sentences. This can provide an occasional useful consolidation of skills already learnt, but does not make full use of the opportunities for learning in the home.

- Homework is most effective when it links to learning within the classroom. Which activities provide a clear link? For example information collected at home can be used in a data handling lesson. Can parents be made aware of the link through newsletters and displays in the classroom during parent consultations? The value of homework will then be reinforced.

- Difficulties arise when children and parents are unsure how to complete a homework task. How can these difficulties be avoided? Contact books or homework diaries may help, and even the school web page could be a future resource. Clear written instructions, along with detailed verbal instructions given to the child are essential. Part of the plenary of the Numeracy lesson can be used to a demonstrate the activity.

- Can homework involve parents in talking about maths or playing mathematical games? This also ensures an opportunity for the child to communicate mathematically, and to use mathematical vocabulary. For example, homework may involve activities such as:

Snakes and Ladders with a difference

Play snakes and ladders with someone at home, but instead of moving the number of spaces on your dice, work out how many more you would have to add to your dice score to make ten, and move that number of spaces.

Think of a Number

Ask someone at home to think of a whole number and tell them that you will read their mind and guess their number.

Ask them to multiply their number with the next biggest whole number.

Then they should subtract the number they first thought of from their answer.

Ask them to tell you their new answer. Their answer should be a square number. Quickly, find the square root of the answer and that will be the first number they thought of.

They will be amazed!

(Why does it always work?)

Some children will not have opportunities to complete activities such as these at home, through no fault of their own. What can be done to minimalise the disadvantages of children who are not able to work with an adult at home? Will there be an opportunity for children who have not played the game at home to do so at school? This may involve organising paired or group work.

Similarly when homework tasks ask children to collect information – for example, about television programme times or supermarket receipts – is there some way of protecting children who are not able to do this because of their home situation?

Of course children and parents are much more likely to complete tasks when they are fun, straightforward and their value is clear.

When you have formed your own opinions about homework, you will need to discuss these with your staff, either formally or informally. Together you should try to agree on the features of effective homework, which may be added to your mathematics policy statement. This should reinforce the school's policy on homework. A letter might then go to parents explaining exactly how you as a staff aim to use homework to enhance children's learning.

Setting and monitoring homework is time consuming, and to sustain the development you aim to promote through homework, you may need to support colleagues from time to time. You could consider providing examples of homework activities which might be used with several year groups. For example, towards Christmas when staff are particularly busy, you might provide an activity where each child takes home an A4 piece of coloured paper and uses it to make the longest paper chain possible. There might be a small prize for the longest chain. The resulting chains can be measured with non-standard and standard units, and the results recorded.

Reflection

Evaluate, perhaps with the rest of the staff, some of the homework ideas in the school's published scheme, or any schemes you may consider purchasing for the school, against your criteria for effective homework.

There are some useful homework resources in published schemes, and within the NNS Professional Development materials. The IMPACT scheme is also an excellent bank of tried ideas for homework. Information on this can be found at the following address:

The IMPACT Project
University of North London
Holloway Road
London N7 8BP

You may also find it useful to read Thompson (1999).

Involving parents in targets for children's learning

Setting targets for children's learning can be a useful strategy to raise standards. You may play a part in co-ordinating the way in which these are communicated to parents.

Informing parents of their children's targets may in itself not be sufficient. Parents also need to know how to support their children in reaching targets. Parents who are not offered other ways to support their children may feel that it is their role simply to test performance.

The NNS offers support in the way of leaflets to send to parents which detail possible targets for each year group, and a selection of activities that parents can use at home. These activities can provide an essential resource for the parents who otherwise would find it difficult to support their children's learning. These leaflets may well suit your school, and can be accessed on www.standards.dfes.gov.uk/numeracy/publications. You may feel they are a suitable starting point, but can be more closely matched to your individual school's needs. With your support, teachers can add activities and targets to them which correspond more closely to their classes. These activities can then be linked with homework set for each class, and could be further supported through packs of games and puzzles available in the school library for parents to borrow.

Reporting to parents

Parental consultations and annual reports are an essential part of the process of involving parents in their children's learning of mathematics. Your role as subject leader in supporting staff may be quite an informal one, but you will want to ensure that these opportunities are used well.

Parental reports and consultations allow teachers to talk about both formative and summative assessment. They can be seen as a time to discuss children's learning targets and negotiate further parental support. Issues surrounding homework can be clarified. Your development of effective assessment of mathematics and target setting across the school will therefore be important. Open and continual communication with parents is essential, particularly in an area such as mathematics where parents may be anxious to help their children in the right way. Parents will want to be informed and involved throughout the year, and not just at its completion.

Reporting to parents should give an indication of children's achievements and areas for development. Parents may also request some data to give them a more objective idea of the children's level of attainment. Standardised scores from QCA tests may be useful here, but would need to be qualified by the teacher's more rounded knowledge of the child's learning. Reporting should not simply describe the areas covered by the curriculum. If this is the case in your school, you could consider giving this information to parents perhaps at the beginning of the term in a newsletter, allowing the use of annual reports and consultations to give more individualised information about the child.

Written reports tend to be summative, but should still be used as an opportunity to set targets for future learning. Again your support here may be quite informal, offering advice, and you could call upon the specific guidance and model reports on the QCA website.

You should be prepared to state the features of effective reporting to parents in mathematics. They could include:

- a summary of significant progress made;
- an idea of how the child's achievements compare with the level expected for the age of the child, using the National Curriculum or National Numeracy Strategy as a benchmark;
- results and data when these can be easily explained to parents;
- targets for future progress, with some practical ideas for parents to use to support their children's learning.

As part of your ongoing audit of the teaching and learning of mathematics in your school, it may be useful to gather parents' comments from staff following parental consultations. There may be significant concerns which are voiced by several parents. For example, parents may note that there seems to be less evidence of written work in children's maths books. If this seems to be a widespread concern, perhaps it is an issue which needs to be addressed in a staff meeting. You may agree as a staff that there should be some record made in the children's books that recognises the range of practical work and games used to enhance children's learning during the numeracy lesson. This may take the form of a short written comment by the teacher or LSA for younger children, or comment made by the older children themselves such as:

Today I played a doubling game. I doubled the numbers by partitioning them, doubling the tens and units, and then adding my answers.

This can be written during the plenary of the lesson, where the children are encouraged to reflect on the lesson, what they learned and the strategies they used. The fact that parents voiced this concern may suggest that you need to inform parents of the way the staff believe children learn mathematics. A short newsletter could explain your views, so that parents know what to expect to see in their children's books, and are persuaded that their children are learning through the wide range of activities you offer them.

Summary

Mathematics is perhaps the subject that causes parents most anxiety, due to significant changes in practices. It is important therefore to ensure that parents are well informed. With knowledge of the way in which they can make a difference to their children's learning, and the confidence which grows from working in partnership with the school, parents can have a very positive impact on their child's learning.

9 HAVING AN IMPACT ON TEACHING AND LEARNING ACROSS THE SCHOOL

➔ The National Standards for Subject Leadership state that subject leaders should:

- have knowledge and understanding of the characteristics of high quality teaching and the main strategies for improving and sustaining high standards of teaching, learning and achievement for all pupils.

Is it possible for you as a subject leader to influence the way mathematics is taught and learned in any classroom other than your own?

Reflection

Have you ever changed your practice because of another member of staff? You may have been inspired by another teacher, perhaps after talking to them informally, or following their input into a staff meeting. Have you ever been on a training course which has caused you to reflect on your own practice, and try new ideas and approaches? Of course, some changes have been imposed on the primary classroom, but an effective training course can convince teachers to choose to change their practice.

As a successful subject leader, you will want to promote certain beliefs and practices, and develop a climate where teachers feel confident to learn from you and from each other, to reflect on their current practice, and to implement critically new ideas and initiatives. This chapter will consider some simple ways in which you might have an impact on classroom practice across the school.

Medium-term planning

Reflection

Consider the school's medium-term plans for mathematics, which may be for a half or a full term. If you were a newly appointed member of staff or an inspector, what would the format of the medium-term plan tell you about the beliefs of the staff?

For example, is the medium-term planning taken from a published scheme? This suggests that the staff rely heavily on the published scheme itself. It may be a very successful scheme, and the staff may need the direct support that the scheme provides. However, if you are trying to promote a move away from the scheme, perhaps a different format for medium-term planning could be considered. If the medium-term planning were taken from the NNS sample plans, teachers would necessarily have a greater input on the way in which the objectives are transformed into lessons and activities, rather than blindly following the scheme. Perhaps this would mean that the needs and interests of individual children and classes would be more closely considered. Some staff may genuinely need the support of the scheme, or may be using the scheme in a very effective way, in which case the medium-term planning could be taken from the NNS but have an extra column to include references to the scheme. The NNS Unit plans may also be useful as a reference.

Week	Topic	Objectives	References to scheme or unit plans
1			
2			
3			
4			
5			
6			

Example 1 of a developed NNS medium-term plan

Where a subject leader is situated in a school where the staff make good use of a scheme or the NNS Unit Plans, but tend to over rely on them, teachers' books from other schemes and reference books can be purchased. References to alternative schemes can be added to medium-term planning, enabling staff to be more selective in their use of published resources. Finding these references may be a task for the subject leader, or staff might work together in year groups to find the references themselves, requiring allocated time in staff meetings.

Week	Topic	Objectives	References to scheme or unit plans	References to other books
1				
2				
3				
4				
5				
6				

Example 2 of a developed NNS medium-term plan

In another situation, a subject leader might be developing links with ICT and mathematics through a series of staff development sessions. The required format for medium-term planning in this case could include ICT links, which again might be inserted by the mathematics or ICT subject leader, the teacher or preferably all of these colleagues working together. Again, time may need to be allocated for this task in a staff meeting.

Week	Topic	Objectives	Possible ICT activities
1			
2			
3			
4			
5			
6			

Example of a medium-term plan with ICT links

Similarly direct references to problem-solving and investigative activities could be required in the medium-term planning where a school has been developing the teaching and learning of the skills of using and applying mathematics found in MAI.

Week	Topic	Objectives	MAI activities
1			
2			
3			
4			
5			
6			

Example of medium-term plan with MAI links

Where a change in the requirements for medium-term planning is implemented, this will need to be negotiated with the head teacher. If the changes signify an increase in paperwork and workload, then time in staff meetings may be needed to support staff.

It is important that the changes in requirements for planning happen after your staff development has taken place, when you work with the staff to reach a shared understanding of the need to modify your current practices. Otherwise the changes will be seen as an unnecessary burden.

Weekly planning

A similar reflection on the requirements for teachers' weekly planning can reveal the shared beliefs and understanding of the staff as to the nature of effective teaching and learning of mathematics. After an inspection and your own auditing and monitoring of mathematics across the school, you might plan to address the development of a particular aspect of the three part lesson. You could then give some informal support to your colleagues and some formal input through a staff meeting or INSET day, as has been discussed in earlier chapters. Following your staff development, you might discuss with the staff a change in the school's format for weekly planning which would reflect the changes you and the staff have agreed to implement.

For example, you might be working with colleagues who are trying to ensure that there is a significant increase in the direct, interactive teaching part of the three part lesson. The following weekly plan which is commonly used would not necessarily support the teachers in this:

Mental and oral objectives	Mental and oral activity	Main objective	Lower achievers	Middle achievers	Higher achievers	Plenary

Example I of weekly plan

The following format requires teachers to plan for their teaching input, which is the most significant part of the lesson.

Mental and oral objectives	Mental and oral activity	Main objective	Teaching input	Lower achievers	Middle achievers	Higher achievers	Plenary

Example 2 of weekly plan

The format above appears to suggest that children will always be grouped by ability. Where a subject leader is supporting teachers in using different types of grouping to support a range of learning and teaching styles, the following format could be trialled:

Mental and oral objective	Mental and oral activity	Main objective	Teaching input	Children's activities and groupings	Plenary

Example 3 of weekly plan

Similarly, the format can change focus by inserting columns, for example requesting planning of key vocabulary, possible misconceptions, resources, or activities for able children. In this way, weekly planning can support your work on specific targets taken from your subject development plan. Monitoring of weekly planning as it is submitted to the head teacher can help you to evaluate the success of your subject development plan. You will not want to increase significantly the workload of your colleagues, but you may change its focus, and therefore ensure that certain aspects of the lesson are highlighted. Your reasons for implementing changes in planning should be discussed and explained to the rest of the staff. Indeed, you should only present such a change after fully discussing issues in staff meetings, so that the staff have a shared understanding of the need for change.

Working with colleagues in the classroom

You may be asked to observe other teachers in their classrooms as part of the school's monitoring policy. Lesson observations provide a rich opportunity for monitoring and developing the teaching and learning of mathematics. There is at present a culture of observation and many teachers are now accustomed to this practice. However, mathematics is an area where a teacher's confidence and subject knowledge may be in need of support, and observations can cause anxiety. Their success therefore will lie in your open relationship with your colleagues and your ability to agree beforehand the features of effective teaching and learning with the whole staff.

I would suggest then that observations are more successful and purposeful when they follow staff development which has established exactly the features of effective teaching and learning. These should be discussed in full, and agreed with the staff, and then could be drawn up into a list or document. Teachers then will be fully familiar with the sorts of features you will be looking for, and how you will judge lessons. Your written comments may refer to these features, and your feedback will be an opportunity to share success, and to suggest ways of moving forward. The agenda for observations will thus be open and shared by the staff as a whole.

A list of features of an effective lesson may suggest that every feature should be present in every lesson. This is clearly unrealistic and inappropriate. The staff should agree that some features would be present in an effective lesson, whilst others would not be suitable. The following list of characteristics of effective three part lessons might be a starting point for your staff discussion. However, any features adopted on your own list should be fully discussed and agreed with your staff. This list can only be a starting point for discussion.

Mental and oral work
Clear start, stating objectives
High expectations
Brisk pace, allowing thinking time
Variety of activities
Rapid recall of known facts
Focus on mental strategies to derive new facts
All children involved
Target questions for individuals/groups
Support staff targeted appropriately
Children explaining their strategies without loss of pace
Accurate use of vocabulary by teacher and children
Mental work linked to the main part of lesson when appropriate or to ongoing targets

The main part of the lesson
Teaching input
Objectives stated and linked to previous and future work
Connectionist teaching
Direct, interactive teaching, modelling mathematics
Demonstration using a variety of good resources
New vocabulary highlighted and use of symbols modelled
Children explaining their strategies
Awareness of possible misconceptions
Targeted questions
Children's effective and efficient methods used as teaching points
(Review homework activity)

Children's activities
Varied classroom organisation to match objectives e.g. whole class, groups, pairs, individual
Manageable, differentiated tasks covering similar content
Teacher to use most of this time for direct teaching with a clear focus
Clear focus for LSA
High expectations in terms of demand and amount of work, behaviour etc.
Emphasis on learning rather than recording
Effective provision and use of resources

Plenary
Sufficient time allowed for and value given to the plenary, with a varied format including some of the following:
Reinforcement of lesson objectives, key facts, vocabulary
Assessment through open, probing questions

Sharing of ideas and strategies
Use of misconceptions as teaching points
Targeted key questions
Reflection on what has been learnt
Application of learning to new contexts
Extension when lesson objectives have been met
Links to future work
(Setting and discussion of homework)

Summary

As subject leader, you will want to implement lasting changes and developments in the practice of your colleagues. To do this takes time and patience, and requires that you work alongside staff, implementing change at their pace, and perhaps negotiating and modifying your own vision during the process. Rushing to impose changes on colleagues who do not share your beliefs and understanding can result in skin-deep changes which are rarely sustained or effective. This book as a whole can be seen as offering ideas for this process, with this chapter suggesting specific ideas.

10 THE POLICY STATEMENT FOR MATHEMATICS

➔ The National Standards for Subject Leadership state that subject leaders should:

- develop and implement policies and practices for the subject which reflect the school's commitment to high achievement, effective teaching and learning;
- develop and implement policies and practices to ensure governors are well informed about subject policies, plans and policies, the success in meeting objectives and targets, and subject-related professional development plans.

Many newly appointed subject leaders are expected to review or rewrite the mathematics policy soon after their appointment. It is important, however, that this is based on a sound knowledge of current practice within the school. Therefore it may be beneficial to leave a review of the policy until you have gathered information about current provision, and have spent some time in the school. Sometimes an inspection or the School Development Plan may require an earlier review of the policy, and in this case the policy may be written and then amended if necessary at a later date. References can be made in the policy to the subject development plan and proposed review of current practices. The process of discussing or writing the policy can in itself provide an opportunity for you as a subject leader to gain an insight into the beliefs and practices of the staff.

It is important to have a clear understanding of the purposes of the policy itself. Policy statements are required for two purposes.

- To represent the shared understanding of the staff as to the nature of mathematics and the characteristics of effective teaching and learning. The policy can be seen as the result therefore of the professional dialogue, informal or formal, which led by the subject leader has resulted in a common agreement on key issues.

- To inform audiences outside the school of this shared understanding. Audiences will include supply teachers, newly appointed staff, governors, parents, representatives from the LEA and OFSTED inspectors.

Writing the policy statement

The first purpose of the policy suggests that the subject leader cannot effectively undertake a review or reworking of the statement in the first few weeks after appointment. The policy represents professional dialogue. The subject leader therefore needs to devote time to understanding current views and practices, and to

implement developments where these are necessary. The writing of the policy statement can be seen as the last stage in the process of development.

A review of the policy should begin with opportunities for discussion, perhaps stimu-
lated by a staff development session if time allows.

You might use open questions to start the discussion:

- What is mathematics and why do we teach it?
- What are the essential parts of mathematics that we want all our children to
  leave our school knowing?
- What is the best way to learn mathematics?
- What is good teaching of mathematics?
- What are the disadvantages of the three part lesson?
- When do we use mathematics in real life?

The actual writing of the statement may also take place in a whole staff meeting, which
can be time consuming, or be undertaken by a representative group of teachers led
by the subject leader, and then presented to the rest of the staff for redrafting.
Where time is limited the subject leader may be in a position to rewrite or amend
the policy statement, following whole school discussion, and present it to the staff in
a staff meeting for redrafting.

Whichever method is most appropriate, it is essential that each member of staff feels
confident to contribute their views to the whole staff discussion of the statement.
This allows the policy to be fully representative. A quieter member of staff may be
approached on an individual basis for their contribution if the subject leader feels
they are unlikely to contribute to large-scale discussions, but the subject leader
should reflect on the way staff discussions are led if such a situation has arisen.

Reflection

*Reflect on the writing of a policy statement for the area of the curriculum where you
are least confident. Does the policy support your teaching in this area? Did you have
an input into its writing?*

OFSTED is an important audience for the policy statement, using this document as
part of their decision making process. The policy is sent to the inspection team
before their visit, and is used to help formulate questions for the inspection. The
policy can provide information about the vision of the staff and how this converges
with the whole school aims. OFSTED is particularly interested in consistency.
Therefore it is important that the mathematics policy works alongside other documents such as the assessment policy, the policy for inclusion etc. Inspections will also
seek to identify whether the views and practices represented in the policy are
shared amongst the whole staff, including the head teacher, LSAs and the governor

responsible for mathematics. Therefore it is essential that the policy does represent the beliefs of the staff as a whole.

What to include in the policy statement

Consideration of the second purpose of the policy, to inform other audiences, can help you to decide what to include in the statement. Most schools include the following.

A statement of the aims of the teaching of mathematics

This is the most important part of the policy as it clearly states the beliefs of the staff as to the nature of mathematics, the characteristics of effective teaching and learning of mathematics and the contribution of mathematics to the whole school mission. This can only be as a result of professional dialogue between members of staff. Although this part of the policy will be shaped by your own beliefs, consistency across the school is very important. As subject leader you will want to promote your own vision, but the policy should reflect the shared understanding of the staff as to the aims of mathematics education.

You may also state your more specific objectives for mathematics education. Here you may refer to coverage of the curriculum for the Foundation Stage and the National Curriculum, through the NNS. You may mention ways in which you have adapted the requirements of the NNS. For example, your school may have a particular belief in investigations and problem solving activities, and have an extended daily mathematics lesson on one day of each week.

The teaching and learning of mathematics

This section will link clearly to your beliefs in the aims of mathematics education, and how these are put into practice. You might make reference here to the NNS, rather than describe in detail elements already documented in the framework. You may also want to mention specific aspects of the teaching of mathematics which are particular to your school. For example, your school may have a special interest in European connections, and this could play an important part in the mathematics curriculum. Or you may have a mathematics trail around the school grounds, or a strong link with mathematics in the community.

This section of your policy statement should also explain briefly your policy relating to:

- planning requirements and the procedures to ensure continuity and progression;
- the way children are grouped for mathematics, e.g. setting;
- the provision for able, gifted and talented children;
- the provision for children with additional needs;
- the way in which calculations are taught;
- the use of LSAs;
- the use of resources, and in particular ICT;

- the use of published schemes;
- cross-curricular learning;
- targets for children's learning;
- homework and the involvement of parents in their children's learning.

Assessment procedures

This is an important part of the policy and should state clearly how assessment is used to inform short-term, medium-term and long-term planning. Strategies for assessment and record keeping should also be described. You will need to address:

- procedures for assessments against key objectives and record keeping requirements;
- procedures for reaching and moderation of teacher assessments against, National Curriculum level descriptors;
- the preparation for and administration of National Tests, and how the information they provide is used to set whole school targets;
- the way in which progress of individual children with additional educational needs is recorded;
- the transfer of information between teachers and schools.

Social, moral, spiritual and cultural development

The policy should state how the teaching and learning of mathematics contributes to children's development in this area. This is an interesting focus for staff discussion, and it may be useful to have some ideas to start such a discussion.

Children's social development may be addressed through the playing of mathematical games, the use of discussion (for example, when sharing mental strategies) and the opportunities for collaborative work. The potential for moral development through mathematics is more difficult to define. It is possible to explore the ways in which right and wrong are sometimes fixed within mathematics, and how this compares with other subjects or aspects of life. Spiritual development may occur when exploring the relationships and patterns within mathematics, which can inspire a feeling of awe and wonder. Mathematics offers many opportunities for the exploration of other cultures, for example the multiplication methods of the Ancient Egyptians, the structure of Japanese numbers or the patterns of Islam. In other senses, mathematics could be seen as culture free. Children with English as an additional language who have previous knowledge of written numbers and mathematical symbols may find that written mathematics is an excellent form of communication in the early days of integration into an English speaking classroom.

Inclusion and equal opportunities

There should be a statement explaining your policy of equal opportunities and commitment to the three principles of inclusion stated in the National Curriculum.

Health and safety

There should be a short statement on health and safety procedures.

Review

Describe when and how the present policy will be reviewed.

Some schools have policy statements for generic areas such as teaching and learning, cross curricular learning etc, and the policy for mathematics can make references to these statements rather than repeating them. The subject leader, along with other members of staff, will want to be involved with the formulation of other policies for areas such as assessment.

Reflection

Reflect on your present policy for mathematics and the way it was formulated. Does it fulfil the two purposes for policies?

Summary

The policy statement should summarise the teaching and learning practices in your school. It should describe current practices, rather than changes you hope to promote in the future, which are recorded in the subject development plan. It should be short, concise and positive in tone. It is a professional document and provides an OFSTED inspector's first impression of your work. You should feel confident that you can talk through each section, and discuss actual practices in your school which exemplify the policy. The statement is the result of your professional planning and development of mathematics throughout your school. In this way it can be seen as evidence of your success as mathematics subject leader.

Anghileri, J. (ed) (2001) *Principles and Practices in Arithmetic Teaching*. Buckingham: Open University Press.

Askew, M., Brown, M., Rhodes, V., Johnson, D. and Wiliam, D. (1997) *Effective Teachers of Numeracy: Report of a Study Carried Out for the Teacher Training Agency*. London: King's College, University of London.

Booth, T., Ainscow, M., Black-Hawkins, K., Vaughan, M. and Shaw, L. (2000) *Index for Inclusion, Developing Learning and Participation in Schools*. Bristol: Centre for Studies on Inclusive Education.

Cooper, B. and Dunne, M. (2000) *Assessing Children's Mathematical Knowledge*. Buckingham: Open University Press.

DfES (1999) *From Thinking Skills to Thinking Classrooms*. www.dfes.gov.uk

DfES (1999) *The National Numeracy Strategy: Framework for Teaching Mathematics from Reception to Year 6*. London: DfES.

DfES/QCA (1999) *The National Curriculum Handbook for Primary Teachers in England*. London: DfES/QCA.

DfES (2000) *Mathematical Challenges for Able Pupils in Key Stages 1 and 2*. London: DfES.

DfES (2001) *Teachers' Standards Framework: Helping You Develop*. www.dfes.gov.uk

DfES (2001) *Towards the National Curriculum for Mathematics: Examples of what pupils with special educational needs should be able to do at each P level*. London: DfES.

DfES (2001) *Using Assess and Review Lessons*. London: DfES.

DfES (2001) *Guidance to Support Pupils with Specific Needs in the Daily Mathematics Lesson*. London: DfES.

DfES (2001) *Using Key Objectives, National Curriculum Level Descriptions and National Curriculum Optional Tests at Key Stages 1, 2 and 3 in Mathematics*. London: DfES.

DfES *Reasoning about Numbers, with Challenges and Simplifications*. www.standards.dfes.gov.uk/numeracy/publications

DfES *Transition from Year 6 to Year 7 Mathematics Units of Work*. www.standards.dfes.gov.uk/numeracy/publications

DfES *Using ICT to Support Mathematics in Primary Schools*. www.standards.dfes.gov.uk/numeracy/publications

DfES *National Numeracy Strategy Professional Development Materials*. www.standards.dfes.gov.uk/numeracy/professional/development

DfES *Mathematical Activities for The Foundation Stage*. www.standards.dfes.gov.uk/numeracy/publications

DfES *Guide for Your Professional Development*. www.standards.dfes.gov.uk/numeracy/publications

Field, K., Holden, P. and Lawlor, H. (2000) *Effective Subject Leadership*. London: Routledge.

Fox, R., Montagne-Smith, A., and Wilkes, S. (2000) *Using ICT in Primary Mathematics*. London: David Fulton.

Hughes, M. (1986) *Children and Number*. Oxford: Basil Blackwell.

Hughes, M., Deforges, C. and Mitchell, C. (2000) *Numeracy and Beyond*. Buckingham: Open University Press.

Koshy, V. (2001) *Teaching Mathematics to Able Children*. London: David Fulton.

Montague-Smith, A. (1997) *Mathematics in Nursery Education*. London: David Fulton.

OFSTED (2000) *The National Numeracy Strategy: an Interim Evaluation by HMI*. London: OFSTED.

OFSTED (2000) *The National Numeracy Strategy: the First Year*. London: OFSTED.

Pound, L. (1999) *Supporting Mathematical Development in the Early Years*. Buckingham: Open University Press.

QCA (1999) *Teaching Mental Calculation Strategies*. London: QCA.

QCA (1999) *Teaching Written Calculations*. London: QCA.

QCA (1999) *Standards in Mathematics*. London: QCA.

QCA (2000) *Bridging Units in Mathematics: Linking Fractions, Decimals and Percentages*. London: QCA.

QCA (2000) *Bridging Units in Mathematics: Algebra: Introducing Symbols*. London: QCA.

QCA (2001) *The Curriculum Guidance for the Foundation Stage*. London: QCA.

QCA (2001) *Planning, Teaching and Assessing the Curriculum for Pupils with Learning Difficulties*. London: QCA.

QCA (2001) *Standards at Key Stage 1 in English and Mathematics*. London: QCA.

QCA (2001) *Standards at Key Stage 2 in English, Mathematics and Science*. London: QCA.

QCA (2001) *Using Assessment to Raise Achievement in Mathematics* www.qca.org.uk

Thompson, I. (ed) (1997) *Teaching and Learning Early Number*. Buckingham: Open University Press.

Thompson, I. (ed) (1999) *Issues in Teaching Numeracy in Primary Schools*. Buckingham: Open University Press.

Wiliam, D. (2001) *Level Best? Levels of Attainment in National Curriculum Assessment*. London: The Association of Teachers and Lecturers.

The IMPACT Project
University of North London
Holloway Road
London
N7 8BP

Web sites

The Association of Teachers of Mathematics	www.atm.org.uk
The Mathematical Association	www.m-a.org.uk
The Department for Education and Skills	www.dfes.gov.uk
The National Numeracy Strategy	www.standards.dfes.gov.uk/numeracy
The Qualifications and Curriculum Authority	www.qca.org.uk
The Office for Standards in Education	www.timss.bc.edu